REMEMBER EMMET:
IMAGES OF THE LIFE AND LEGACY
OF ROBERT EMMET

REMEMBER EMMET:
images of the life and legacy
of Robert Emmet

Ruán O'Donnell

Wordwell

in association with

The National Library of Ireland

First published 2003
Wordwell Ltd
PO Box 69, Bray, Co. Wicklow
Copyright © The author

Cover design: Rachel Dunne.

Cover image: *The trial of Robert Emmet. Born at Dublin in 1778, Died September 20, 1803* (NLI, EP EMME-RO (19) IV).

ISBN 1 869857 59 3

British Library Cataloguing-in-Publication Data.
A catalogue record for this book is available from the British Library.

Typeset in Ireland by Wordwell Ltd.
Repro: Andrew Gregory and Niamh Power.
Editor: Aisling Flood.

Book design: Nick Maxwell and Rachel Dunne.

Printed by Zure S.A., Bilbao.

Published in association with the National Library of Ireland.

For Maeve

Contents

Foreword

Drawn from the Prints and Drawings, Printed Books, Manuscripts, Newspapers, Periodicals and Official Publications collections, the extensive and varied material in the care of the National Library provides a framework and much of the content for this richly illustrated bicentennial publication. Some of the material selected will be familiar to many readers, while other items, for example the embroidered map of Ireland attributed to Sarah Curran, come for the first time into the public domain.

Remember Emmet: images of the life and legacy of Robert Emmet is part of the National Library's continuing programme of publications designed to focus attention on the great storehouse of treasures that the Library contains. Until such time as our new exhibition areas come into being in 2004, we are concentrating much of our outreach policy on publications such as this and, of course, on the ongoing development of access via our web site to library material, particularly items from the Prints and Drawings and Photographs collections.

Whether familiar or previously unknown, the 250 images in this publication—illustrative of the life and legacy of Robert Emmet—have been selected by Dr Ruán O'Donnell and are linked by his scholarly narrative. The Library is grateful to Dr O'Donnell for undertaking this project for us with such enthusiasm and commitment, and we are grateful also to Nick Maxwell of Wordwell for so readily agreeing to co-publish with us. Dr O'Donnell's selection of material from the Library's collections is complemented by some key illustrations drawn from the collections of other institutions, whose kind cooperation we gratefully acknowledge.

Brendan O Donoghue
Director
National Library of Ireland

Preface

Robert Emmet has been an intriguing and enigmatic figure since his exposure to public view in July 1803. He was admired by Republican contemporaries and elevated to iconic status by those who accepted his famous challenge to vindicate his revolutionary ideals. Emmet's position in Irish history, however, was simultaneously adversely affected by widespread ignorance concerning the Rising of 1803. Highly negative impressions of the failed revolt were cultivated by a government keen to minimise the prospect of French military intervention in Ireland, as had been sought by Emmet and other leaders of the United Irishmen. Moreover, the expectation of decisive French assistance before 1815 disposed surviving insurgent commanders to maintain their silence on significant aspects of the 1802–3 conspiracy. Emmet's role in negotiations with Napoleon Bonaparte and the planning stages of a thoroughly feasible Dublin-centred *coup d'état* was treated with predictable scorn in the state-controlled press. Champions of his reputation, most notably childhood friend Thomas Moore, subsequently concentrated on romantic aspects of Emmet's short life in preference to a problematic subversive career that commenced in 1796 and terminated seven years later in martyrdom. Few details of historical value, therefore, came to light before the mid-1800s. By then, pathos stemming from Emmet's relationship with the tragic Sarah Curran and his comparative youth and stoicism when on trial in September 1803 had contributed to the creation of a simplistic, if enduring, view of the Dubliner that obscured his political importance. This distorted profile resulted in Emmet's name and image being very well known in 1903 while the rationale and nature of his activities remained obscure. This bicentennial perspective draws primarily on the extensive collections of the National Library of Ireland, the National Gallery, the National Archives, the National Museum and Kilmainham Gaol to reassess Emmet's life and legacy. Documents, images and items in the possession of the Emmet family, the American Irish Historical Society (New York) and the Royal Irish Academy have also been included thanks to the generous cooperation of the custodians.

Dr Ruán O'Donnell
University of Limerick
June 2003

Acknowledgements

The author wishes to thank the following for their assistance in the production of this book: Brendan O Donoghue, Nick Maxwell, Colette O'Flaherty, Catriona Crowe, Pat Cooke, Labhras Joye, Anne Hodge, Avice-Claire McGovern, and William Cobert. I am also indebted to Joanna Finegan, David Monaghan, Valerie Dowling, Rachel Dunne, Andrew Gregory, Brian Cleary, A. Bonar Law, Geoffrey Croft, Matthew Cains, Nicola Ralston, Louise Holden, Roy Hewson, Josephine McGlade, Niamh O'Sullivan, Siobhán O'Rafferty, Margaret Flood, Michael O'Flanagan, Seán Goff, Con Brogan, Philip Emmet and family, Aisling Flood, Angus Mitchell, Bernadette Cunningham, Kevin Whelan, Tom Bartlett, John Logan, Bernadette Whelan, Lillis O'Laoire, Diarmuid Coogan, Shane MacThomais, Gerry Long, Noel Kissane, Louise Morgan, Scott Kelly, Ted O'Reilly, Frank Connolly, John Gray, Sylvie Kleinman, John Mulcahy, Greg O'Connor, Della Murphy, Al and June O'Donnell, Maurice Kirwan, Kieran Swords, Liam Chambers, Nicholas Carolan, Liam O'Dochartaigh, Colonel Donal O'Carroll, Damien Kiberd, Teresa Kelly, Mel Fearon, Marie McFeely, Helen Carey, Eddy Byrne, Mike King, Anthony Russell, Henry Cairns, John Nolan, Paula Williams, Stephen O'Connell, Jim Quinn, Bernard Browne, Peter Burrowes and the Robert Emmet Association.

Abbreviations

AIHS: American Irish Historical Society

Dúchas: Dúchas, The Heritage Service

Kilmainham: Kilmainham Gaol, Dublin

NAI: National Archives of Ireland

NGI: National Gallery of Ireland

NLI: National Library of Ireland

NMI: National Museum of Ireland

PRO: Public Records Office, London

RIA: Royal Irish Academy

TCD: Trinity College Dublin

Chapter 1

Family, childhood and education

Robert Emmet, one of the most popular and important Irish revolutionaries, was born in Dublin on 4 March 1778. While this urban background had great bearing on his role in Irish history, he was the first male child in the family to reach adulthood in the capital. Emmet's paternal ancestors arrived in Munster from Lancashire, England, in the 1600s and by the late 1700s were present in Tipperary, Limerick, Cork and Kerry. Dr Robert Emmet, father of the rebel leader, hailed from Tipperary Town and in November 1760 married Elizabeth Mason of Ballydowney, Kerry, in Cork City. This connected the increasingly wealthy Emmets to several ancient Irish families in the province, where they acquired numerous small properties through purchase and inheritance. The shift to Dublin was occasioned by Dr Emmet's appointment to the prestigious and lucrative post of State Physician in 1770, and the family moved to 35 Molesworth Street, convenient to the Royal College of Surgeons. By early 1777 the Emmets of Dublin lived in a large building subdivided as 109–110 St Stephen's Green West, where Robert Emmet was born. He was delivered in succession to several children bearing the same name who did not survive infancy. His surviving elder siblings were Christopher Temple and Thomas Addis, born in Cork, and Mary Anne, who was born in Dublin. Their presence in the growing metropolis attracted relatives from the Mason, Temple and, later, Patten families.

The early life of Robert Emmet was spent in the south city of Dublin, where he was destined to meet a premature and violent death in 1803. He attended the elite primary school run by the Edwards brothers in Dopping Court and proceeded to the famous English Grammar School founded by Samuel Whyte in 75 (later 79) Grafton Street. Whyte's 'academy' produced such notable graduates as the playwright Richard Brinsley Sheridan, and its master frequently brought students to perform in Crow Street Theatre. Emmet would have met Thomas Moore of Aungier Street, who, as Ireland's premier lyricist of the nineteenth century, did much to immortalise his tragic contemporary. School and home instruction gave Emmet fluency in French and Latin when a youth and inculcated in him a strong sense of civic duty and activism. His extant juvenilia proves that Emmet engaged in the family practice of writing patriotic poetry, as did his primary educator, Whyte. Emmet's schoolbooks were heavily annotated with margin comments, diagrams and drawings that testified to a broad range of scholarly reading and deep comprehension. From his earliest days, mathematics, oratory, chemistry and political philosophy were practised by Emmet with the acumen typical of the scion of a family in which genius was the norm.

The coincidence of Emmet's childhood with the pivotal American War of Independence was clearly significant, given his later actions and the common perception of shared transatlantic political conditions. The often insane King George III was widely regarded by his Irish and American subjects as the personification of repression, nepotism and atavism. The revolt of the 'Patriots' touched the young Emmet through the pro-American sympathies of his father and reinforced pre-existing nationalist proclivities that pervaded the family. The consequences of the struggle became very apparent when their Boston-based Temple relatives abandoned the new republic for the Emmet home on St Stephen's Green. This migration facilitated the marriage of Christopher Temple Emmet to Anne Western Temple, a second cousin, in September 1784, and the couple moved into nearby 25 York Street two years later. Temple Emmet was in the early stages of what promised to be a brilliant legal career when struck down by smallpox on the Munster Circuit in early 1788. This dealt the family a profound shock and disposed Thomas Addis to turn his back on the medical practice for which he had qualified in Edinburgh in 1784 and to opt instead for training as a barrister in Dublin and London. Although an able lawyer and Attorney-General of New York State in 1812, Addis Emmet had made what many would have regarded as a flawed decision given his father's unrivalled access to medical patronage.

By 1790, when the French Revolution of July 1789 was consolidated in Paris, the drive for representative government in Ireland was gathering pace. A series of Relief Acts had begun to dismantle the hated 'Penal laws' but failed to redress the underlying causes of Irish disaffection. More importantly, it became increasingly obvious that the prevailing attitude in London and Dublin would not countenance the full emancipation of the oppressed majority population. This was highly dangerous, given the international appeal of the 'rights of man' in a period when two revolutions had established the latent power of the masses against corrupt monarchies. Robert Emmet attended the historic 1790 hustings in Dublin to observe his father engage the main reform leader and city candidate, Henry Grattan, in a public defence of his bona fides. Grattan, an acquaintance of the Emmets, was astounded when the twelve-year-old Robert afterwards recited an essay on the theme of liberty, as was its author, Dr William Drennan. Grattan was returned to the House of Commons at College Green, along with Henry Fitzgerald, brother of the ill-fated Lord Edward Fitzgerald. The two new MPs entered Parliament with the aim of obliging the bastion of the Ascendancy to extend the franchise to all adult males, to reduce the authority of Westminster in Ireland and to redress the artificially degraded position of Catholics and Presbyterians in Irish society.

Drennan was a medical colleague of Dr Emmet's who, with Theobald Wolfe Tone, Samuel Neilson, Thomas Russell, James Napper Tandy and other advanced radicals, founded the Society of United Irishmen in Dublin and Belfast in October/November 1791. Their objective was to institute a French- or American-style democratic government in Ireland in place of the sectarian Commons and Dublin Castle executive, where real power was vested in administrators appointed in London. Such matters were discussed in depth in St Stephen's Green, where Addis Emmet had returned in 1790, having befriended Tone in London. Tone, Drennan, Russell *et al.* were frequent guests in the Emmet family home, located around the corner from Leinster House, the city base of the influential Fitzgeralds. Robert Emmet, a product of his extraordinary times, was consequently close to the heart of Irish radicalism when still in his adolescence. His progression into revolutionary politics in adulthood was not inevitable but, nonetheless, a natural, explicable and consistent step for someone of his background.

Robert Emmet by **John Comerford** (NGI, 7341).

Waterford miniaturist John Comerford produced the best likeness of Robert Emmet from sketches committed to brown paper when his subject was tried on 19 September 1803. Comerford was evidently commissioned by Emmet and delivered the finished watercolour-on-ivory portrait to his family.

City of Cork (1799) by Thomas S. Roberts (NLI, ET 198 TB).

The marriage of Dr Robert Emmet to Elizabeth 'Betty' Mason consolidated the extensive Munster connections of the Tipperary Emmets. Their children were related to many prominent families in Kerry, Cork and Limerick, including several of Catholic and Gaelic origin.

When living in Cork in the 1760s, the Emmets acquired properties at Inchigeela, Dooneny, Derreenvealnaslee, Cottage, Dunscombe's March and Hammond's Marsh.

Terms	Landlords Rent	To whom Set & Terms	Yearly Rents	Profit Rents
lives renewable for ever	£ 27.19.1	Timothy Quilinan for 21 years from 5 April 1776	£ 143.15.0	£ 115.15.11
farm Grant	62.1.3	Set to Moses Dawson dec.d for 3 lives from March 1779	165:0:0	102.18.9
three Lives	. . . .	Set to James Reardan dec.d for three lives renewable for ever	11.5.0	. . . .
	. . . .	Rev.d William Armstrong for 31 years from March 1770	4.6.0	. . . .
able for ever	30.15.0	Thomas Connors for 30 years from April 1772	18.9.0	. . . .
			34.0.0	33.5.0

Total profit Rent to be Divided into Two parts .... £ 221.19.8

Mrs Emmets half thereof Devised by her to Doctor Emmitt .... £ 110.19.10

As the Doctor has a Copy of the Will I have underneath sent only a short abstract.

"I give all and every my freehold Messuages Lands Tenements and Hereditaments Situate lying
by the Names of Raheen part of Kyle and Crossoil and Bohercrow each and every of them To Hold
to the use of Thomas Addis Emmett Esq.r & his Heirs Male, Remainder to Robert Emmth &
Remainder to the Right Heirs of the s.d Robert Emmett the Elder"

The Emmets of Munster (NAI, Rebellion Papers, 620/15/2/1).

Dr Robert Emmet (Dúchas/Emmet family).

The Emmets remained in close contact with their country relatives and
business associates after moving to Dublin in 1770. Bolstered by
income from inheritance and his various medical salaries, Dr Emmet
acquired 2 Palace Street and other city investments that generated
rents. His Tipperary interests were generally attended to by lawyer
Richard Sadlier.

Steeven's Hospital **by Robert Pool, engraved by John Cash** (NLI, ET
708 TA).

Thomas Addis Emmet **by Louis François Aubry, mezzotint engraved by T.W. Huffam** (NGI, 11,171).

Christopher Temple Emmet (Dúchas/Emmet family).

Christopher Temple and Thomas Addis Emmet, the two eldest children to survive infancy, were both born in Cork and educated in Dublin. Christopher was a gifted student and debater at Trinity College Dublin and practised as a barrister on the Munster Circuit from 1781 until stricken with fatal illness in 1788. He was survived by his widow Anne and daughter Catherine ('Kitty'). On going to London to study law, Addis Emmet met Theobald Wolfe Tone, with important consequences.

***Mary Anne Emmet* by Thomas Hickey** (Kilmainham).

Although not permitted to attend Trinity College owing to her gender, Mary Anne Emmet shared her family's interest in politics and was acquainted with the Irish circle of Mary Wollstonecraft and William Godwin.

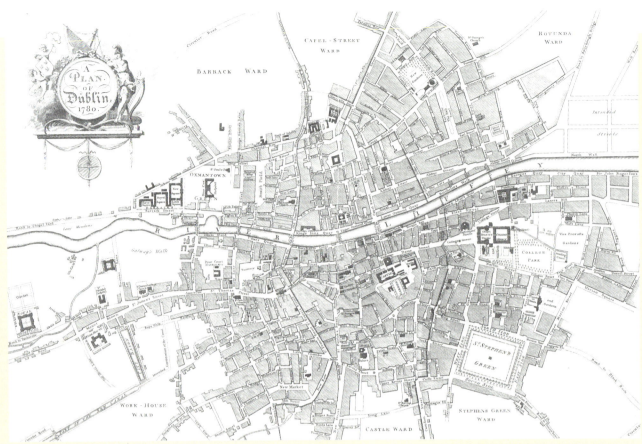

Map of Dublin in 1780 **by Robert Pool and John Cash**
(courtesy of A. Bonar Law).

The relocation of the Emmets to the fashionable and expanding south side of the capital testified to their increasing social status and wealth. The spacious house occupied by the family on St Stephen's Green (facing page) was adjacent to the Royal College of Surgeons and sufficiently large to accommodate visiting relatives. The house, to the right of the college, was divided into numbers 109 and 110 after the marriage of Addis Emmet to Jane Patten in St Mary's Church, Dublin, in June 1791.

St. Stephen's Green, Dublin **by James Malton** (NLI, PD 3181 TX 143).

Emmet family bible
(RIA, MS 12.G.14).

Residence of Dr Emmet and his son
(Dúchas/Emmet family).

The birth of Robert Emmet on Ash Wednesday, 4 March 1778, was listed in the family bible. He was baptised the following week in St Peter's and St Kevin's Church, Aungier Street. This seventeeenth-century bible was owned by Dr T.A. Emmet, grandnephew of the revolutionary.

The Lisburn and Lambeg Volunteers firing a feu de joie in the Market Square in Lisburn, in honour of the Convention of 1782 by John Carey (NLI, HP (1782) 2).

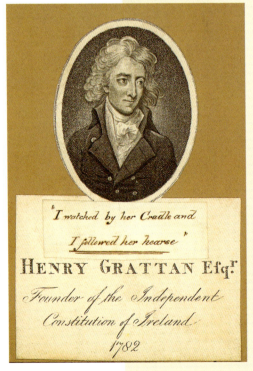

"I watched by her Cradle and I followed her hearse"

HENRY GRATTAN Esqr.

Founder of the Independent Constitution of Ireland 1782

Henry Grattan Esqr. Founder of the Independent Constitution of Ireland (*Dublin Magazine*, December 1799).

The crisis caused by the American War of Independence was exploited by advocates of Parliamentary reform led by Irish 'Patriot' Henry Grattan, an Emmet family acquaintance. Pro-reform sympathy within the paramilitary Volunteers increased the bargaining power of Grattan's followers in Westminster. The Volunteers were a civilian militia raised to defend Irish shores from the French. Ulster units were encouraged to back Catholic Emancipation by Revd William Steel Dickson, William Todd Jones and other Northern radicals.

11

Revd Walter Blake Kirwan (*Walker's Hibernian Magazine*, December 1787).

English-born Sir Edward Newenham, a confidant of Dr Emmet's, was one of the main Dublin-based supporters of American democracy. He and Revd Walter Blake Kirwan, the famed ex-Jesuit turned charity preacher, were frequent dinner guests in St Stephen's Green. The Emmets supported the perspective of the revolting colonists.

Crow Street Theatre (NGI, 2691).

Samuel Whyte Esq. by Hugh Douglas Hamilton, engraved by Henry Brocas, Snr (NLI, BR 2034 TX 9).

13

Robert Emmet (Emmet, *Memoir*).

Robert Emmet progressed from the juvenile academies of
his early years to Samuel Whyte's English Grammar
School on Grafton Street. Whyte embraced the nationalist
spirit abroad in the 1780s and brought his students to
Crow Street Theatre to perform as extras.

James Napper Tandy, **artist unknown** (NGI, 429).

Theobald Wolfe Tone **by Catherine Sampson Tone, engraved by C. Hullmandel** (NLI, EP TONE-TH (2) 1).

Samuel Neilson by Charles Byrne, engraved by **T.W. Huffam** (NGI, 10,646).

15

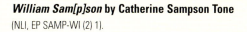

William Sam[p]son by Catherine Sampson Tone
(NLI, EP SAMP-WI (2) 1).

James Napper Tandy, a veteran proto-Republican, was one of the first Dublin-based radicals to coalesce with the nascent United Irishmen in 1790/1791. Belfast-born Dr William Drennan made an important contribution to the ideology, nomenclature and *modus operandi* of the proposed society, which was welcomed by the Presbyterian Belfast radicals adhering to Samuel Neilson. Tone's friends, Thomas Russell of Cork and William Sampson of Derry, were also highly influential, as was Thomas Addis Emmet. They were exasperated by moderation of the Catholic Committee and Whig Clubs in the light of the French Revolution of July 1789. The sinews of the Dublin–Belfast axis thus pre-dated the formal emergence of the United Irishmen in October/November 1791.

The Parliament House, Dublin by **James Malton** (NLI, PD 3181 TX 43).

The main entrance of Trinity College Dublin, opposite the House of Commons, faced down Dame Street.

Emmet, aged fifteen, entered Trinity on 7 October 1793 after being prepared by Revd Lewis of Camden Street. Under the tutorship of Revd Graves, Emmet displayed terrific academic potential. Childhood drawings on copybooks and textbooks evince his lifelong interest in military affairs. Emmet excelled at mathematics and chemistry but never graduated owing to the effects of the French Revolutionary Wars on Ireland.

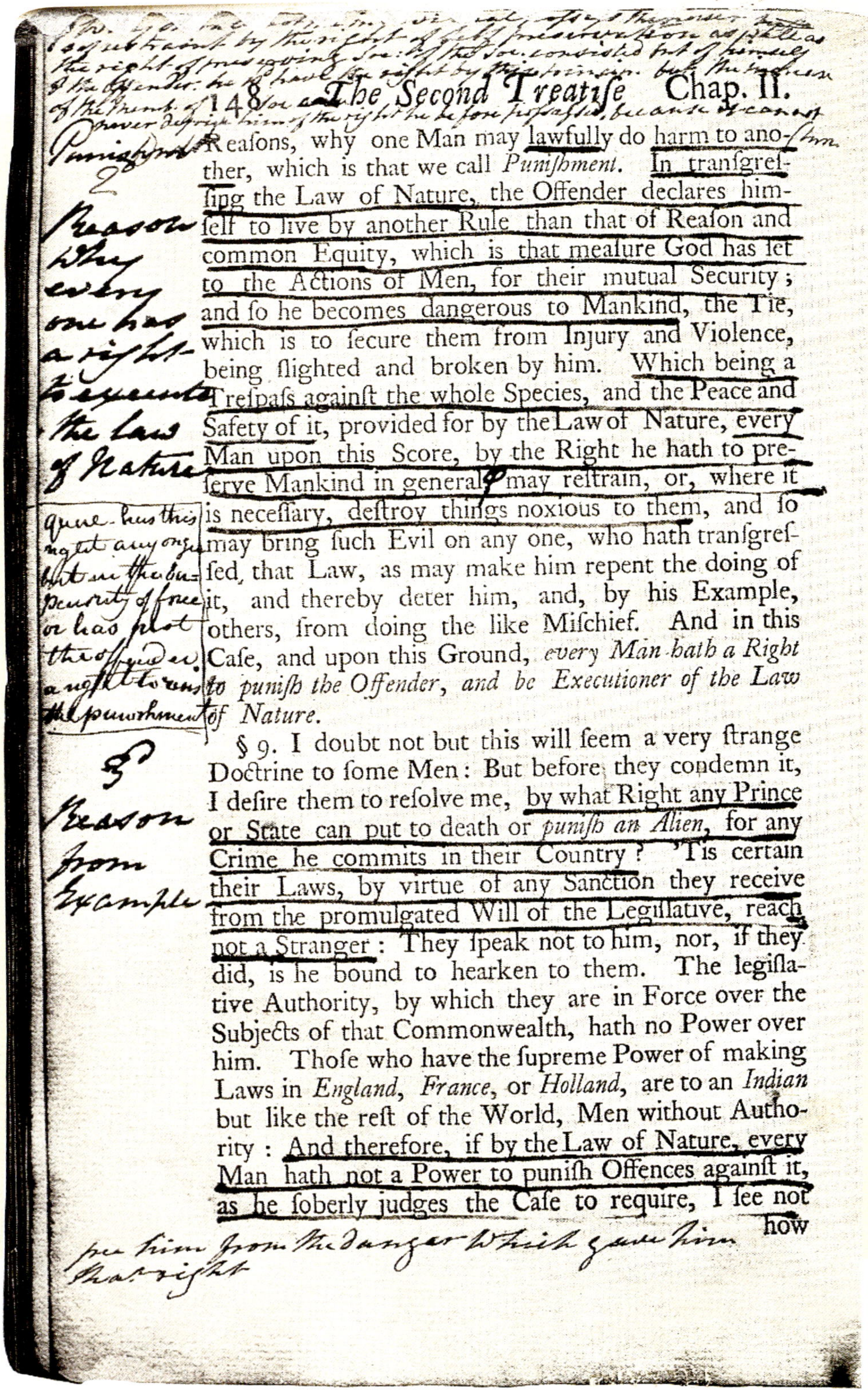

[handwritten notes at top margin, largely illegible]

The Second Treatise   Chap. II.

148

Reasons, why one Man may lawfully do harm to another, which is that we call *Punishment*. In transgressing the Law of Nature, the Offender declares himself to live by another Rule, than that of Reason and common Equity, which is that measure God has set to the Actions of Men, for their mutual Security; and so he becomes dangerous to Mankind, the Tie, which is to secure them from Injury and Violence, being slighted and broken by him. Which being a Trespass against the whole Species, and the Peace and Safety of it, provided for by the Law of Nature, every Man upon this Score, by the Right he hath to preserve Mankind in general, may restrain, or, where it is necessary, destroy things noxious to them, and so may bring such Evil on any one, who hath transgressed that Law, as may make him repent the doing of it, and thereby deter him, and, by his Example, others, from doing the like Mischief. And in this Case, and upon this Ground, *every Man hath a Right to punish the Offender, and be Executioner of the Law of Nature.*

§ 9. I doubt not but this will seem a very strange Doctrine to some Men: But before they condemn it, I desire them to resolve me, by what Right any Prince or State can put to death or *punish an Alien*, for any Crime he commits in their Country? 'Tis certain their Laws, by virtue of any Sanction they receive from the promulgated Will of the Legislative, reach not a Stranger: They speak not to him, nor, if they did, is he bound to hearken to them. The legislative Authority, by which they are in Force over the Subjects of that Commonwealth, hath no Power over him. Those who have the supreme Power of making Laws in *England*, *France*, or *Holland*, are to an *Indian* but like the rest of the World, Men without Authority: And therefore, if by the Law of Nature, every Man hath not a Power to punish Offences against it, as he soberly judges the Case to require, I see not how

[marginal handwritten notes: "Punishment", "Reason why every one has a right to execute the law of Nature", "Reason from Example", and others largely illegible]

17

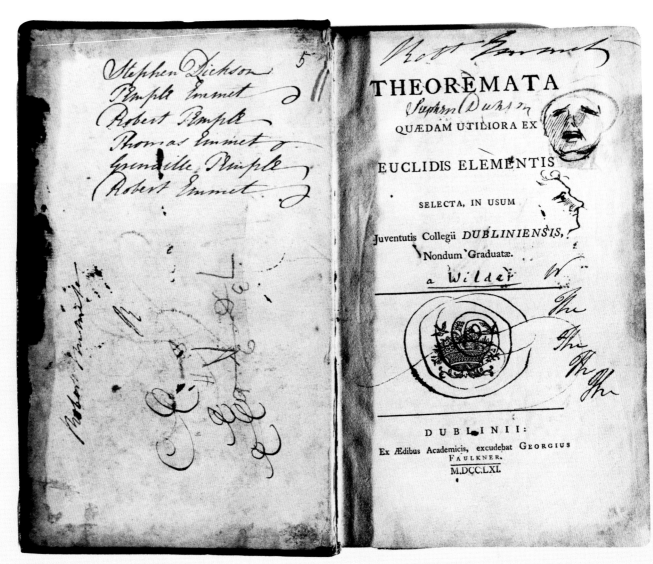

Emmet's textbook
(Dúchas/Emmet family).

Detail from Emmet's textbook (Dúchas/Emmet family).

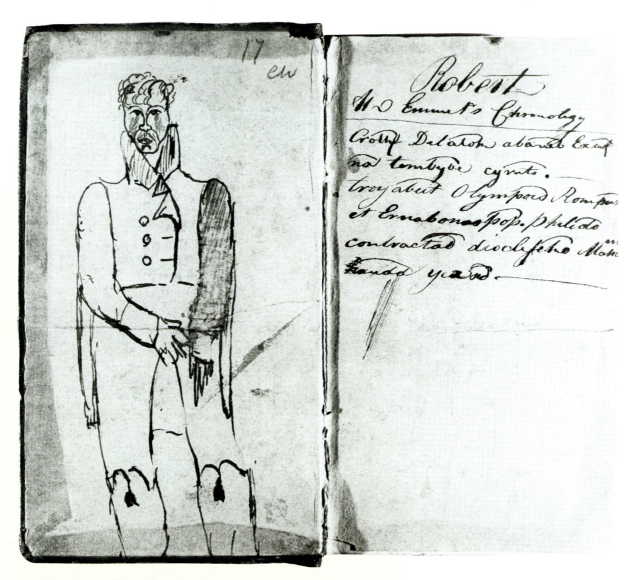

Emmet's textbook
(Dúchas/Emmet family).

Chapter 2

United Irishmen 1791–98

The United Irishmen were originally a legal and largely middle-class body pledged to achieve constitutional reform by means of propaganda and persuasion. Their drive to unite 'Protestant, Catholic and Dissenter [Presbyterian]' and mooted abolition of both sectarian and hereditary privilege were highly ambitious, as was the organisation's aim to 'break the connection' with England. Sovereign independence was deemed absolutely necessary by the United Irishmen, who did not believe that the democratisation of Irish society would be tolerated in Westminster. Ireland was viewed in colonial terms as a resource of military manpower, trade and finance in times of peace and as a major strategic liability in times of war. Britain's declaration of war on France in early 1793, therefore, gravely threatened Irish Republicans, whose capacity for legal popular mobilisation was drastically curtailed by an administration that had learned the lessons of the American War. The rise in 1792–3 of the Defenders, an oath-bound mass movement of pro-French paramilitaries, unleashed a comprehensive counter-insurgent offensive in which the United Irishmen were soon enmeshed. The Defenders violently resisted the implementation of the Militia Act in 1793 and endured hundreds of casualties in support of objectives akin to those of the United Irishmen.

Thomas Addis Emmet was called upon to represent Defender paramilitary suspects facing capital charges and, in November 1792, United Irish colleagues such as Napper Tandy, who had close dealings with subversives. William Drennan, Archibald Hamilton Rowan and several others known to the Emmets were soon implicated. Constrained by wartime bans on public meetings, raising private militias and seditious expressions, the United Irishmen were prevented from marshalling extra-Parliamentary popular forces and began to regard the Defenders as a vehicle for revolutionary change. While moderate elements withdrew from politics, the majority of United Irish leaders were favourably disposed to the April 1794 offer of a French invasion force to facilitate the transition to democracy. Decisive military intervention from France was grasped as the only way forward. Wolfe Tone, however, was compromised during crucial negotiations with the French agent in Dublin, and the pretext of their liaison was used to proscribe the United Irishmen. Preparations were immediately made for the militants to regroup as an emphatically revolutionary body, and in May 1795 a new constitution was adopted to restructure the organisation as auxiliaries to their French allies.

The tenor of United Irish propaganda in Neilson's *Northern Star* became increasingly assertive, spurred by the brutal suppression of the Connacht Defenders and the sacking of the liberal Viceroy Earl Fitzwilliam in 1795. Tone, exiled to America, migrated from Philadelphia to Paris to press the French government to invade at the earliest opportunity. Before leaving Ireland, Tone consulted with Addis Emmet in Rathfarnham, County Dublin, where the lawyer maintained an office and rural home in Butterfield Lane. Tone also conferred in Belfast with Neilson, Henry Joy McCracken and Charles Teeling, who comprised a resolute leadership cadre. Tone's diplomacy in Paris was highly successful, and, while the expeditionary army and its fleet of transports assembled in the Atlantic ports, the reinvigorated United Irishmen extended their reach from their Belfast hub throughout Ulster. The Dublin-based Executive Directory, meanwhile, forged significant connections with the Defenders after May 1795 and prepared a recruitment drive in the provinces. Oath-bound cells created at parish, barony and county level were linked to the capital by specially appointed provincial delegates. Officers were elected every three months and advanced to superior committees, which, in the case of Ulster, were poised to act when the promised French fleet arrived off the Cork coast in late December 1796.

Robert Emmet turned eighteen in 1796 and in December of that year joined the United Irishmen. He had entered Trinity College Dublin three years earlier. Emmet thrived as an undergraduate and formed many new friendships of political importance, not least with Thomas Moore, Michael Farrell and William Corbett. He distinguished himself in the examinations of June 1795. As the political crisis of the 1790s deepened, Emmet balanced his studies with attendance at student debates that attracted John Sheares and other prominent United Irishmen known to his family. Although the long-awaited French fleet was unable to land in December 1796 owing to adverse weather conditions, the presumption that it would return provided a massive boost to United Irish expansion. Addis Emmet joined the Directory in January 1797.

Lord Camden's hard-line government, aided by martial law and the new civilian yeomanry, deployed the military in suspected parts of Ulster in March 1797. Strong measures were applied to disrupt the burgeoning Republican movement.

As the United Irishmen refocused on building up their numbers in the strategic counties of Leinster, Robert Emmet played a leading part in spreading the conspiracy in Trinity, where elite cells were formed. He contributed radical verse to *The Press*, the last newspaper of the United Irishmen, and risked censure by alluding to despotism in college debates in which his talent for oratory was very apparent. Emmet's creative talents were drawn upon in other ways, and he designed a series of seals for the United Irishmen, one of which was later engraved on an emerald family heirloom. His activities were scrutinised on 19–22 April 1798 when Dr Patrick Duigenan and Lord Clare commenced a 'Visitation' aimed at rooting out sedition. This followed closely upon the arrest of much of the United Irish leadership at Oliver Bond's Dublin home on 12 March and the concurrent seizure of Addis Emmet in St Stephen's Green. The Visitation was boycotted by Robert Emmet and Michael Farrell but comprised approximately fifty students, nineteen of whom were formally expelled. Emmet had already left college in anticipation of disgrace and was keeping a low profile to avoid an arrest warrant.

Martial law was stepped up in Leinster and Munster in April, leading to intense pressure on the surviving leaders attached to Lord Edward Fitzgerald and Samuel Neilson to mount a rebellion without the French. It was feared that the number of arrests and arms finds would soon destroy the organisation and that a major showing of the rebels would encourage the French to set sail without delay. In the event, Fitzgerald was arrested on 19 May and Neilson on 23 May, just as the unilateral contingency was being reluctantly initiated. None were aware that the French army intended for Ireland had just been diverted to Egypt. Emmet attended a meeting of rebel officers on 23 May in Abbey Street, one of a number of groups who waited for final orders that never came owing to a last-minute intelligence breakthrough that enabled Dublin Castle to pre-empt the revolutionaries. Although minor skirmishes broke out in and around the city, the vast majority of those who rallied on the first night melted away without detection.

The east front of Trinity College by Robert Pool, engraved by John Lodge (NGI, 10,041 (8)).

Trinity College Dublin, long a bastion of the Protestant Ascendancy, was opened to unprecedented levels of Catholic enrolment by the 1793 Relief Act. Emmet's study of John Locke, William Godwin, Voltaire and other political writers was counterpointed by significant reforms that fell short of fundamental civil rights. The rise of the Defenders undermined the status quo that students of Emmet's generation were meant to maintain.

Trinity College by Robert Pool, engraved by John Cash (NLI, IR 914122).

23

At the late Quarterly Examinations held in our Univerfity, the following young gentlemen obtained Præmiums :

Dobls,	✝ Ardagh,	Roe,
Bradford,	Quarry,	M ffe,
Allman,	Naly,	Mr jackfon,
Lane, 2dus.	Mr. Bennett, fen.	Mr. Wo fe,
Mr. Deane, fen.	Miller, jun.	Burke,
Mr. Carew,	Curran,	Maunfell, jun.
Mayhen,	✝ Emmett,	Caldwell, jun.
Gore,	Mannin,	Rich rds.

At the fame time the following young Gentle men obtained Certificates :

Hamilton, 2dus.	Gordon, 2dus.	Murphy, 3tius.
Mafon, fen.	Dickfon, 1mus.	Robinfon, 4tus.
Morres,	Keatinge,	Mr. Monfell,
Mr. Roe, fen.	Mr. Bennett, 2dus.	Fitzgerald, 6tus.
Gordon, 1mus.	Hamilton, 5tus.	Ulfon,
Magrath,	Mafon, jun.	Wade, jun.
Mc. Cartney,	Donovan.	Sander.

Emmet at Trinity (*Faulkner's Dublin Journal*, 30 June 1795).

William James MacNeven, **artist unknown** (NLI, IR 920041 M11).

William Corbet [sic] **engraved by T.W. Huffam** (NLI, EP CORB-WI (1).

Emmet joined the United Irishmen in December 1796 before news that a French invasion fleet was off the coast of Cork. Thomas Moore of 12 Aungier Street, a childhood friend who protested the dismissal of the liberal Viceroy Earl Fitzwilliam in 1795, joined the revolutionary cells that elected Emmet a leader. The full extent of Emmet's dealings with William Corbett of Cork, Michael Farrell of Longford *et al.* did not come to light for years but confirmed his liaison with senior United Irishmen Dr William James MacNeven and John Chambers. Emmet's renowned contributions to the debates of the College Historical Society marked him as one of the most promising and controversial students of the 1790s. Emmet and Moore used pseudonyms when contributing patriotic verse and articles to *The Press*, a United Irish newspaper published by John Stockdale in Abbey Street until its proscription in March 1798.

Thomas Moore, artist unknown (NLI, EP MOOR-TH (9A) 1).

25

General Lazare
Hoche (NGI, 10,877).

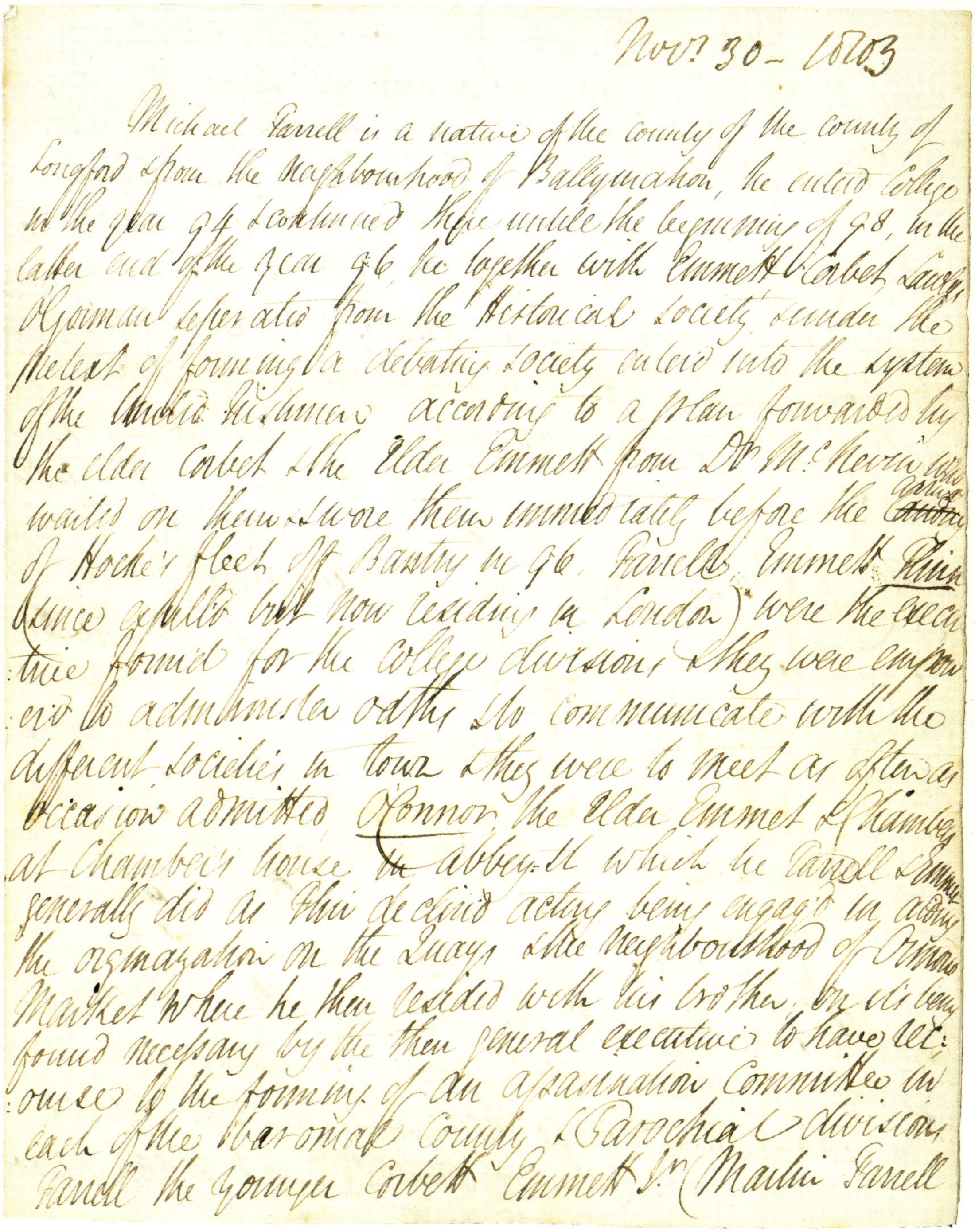

Novr 30 – 1803

Michael Farrell is a native of the county of the county of Longford & from the neighbourhood of Ballymahon, he entered College in the year 94 & continued there untill the beginning of 98, in the latter end of the year 96 he together with Emmett & Corbet, Lawless, O'Gorman seperated from the Historical Society & under the pretext of forming a debating society entered into the system of the United Irishmen according to a plan forwarded by the elder Corbet & the Elder Emmett from Dr McNeven who waited on them & swore them immediately before the coming of Hoche's fleet off Bantry in 96. Farrell, Emmett, Flinn (since expelled but now residing in London) were the executive formed for the college division, & they were empowered to administer oaths & to communicate with the different societies in town & they were to meet as often as occasion admitted O'Connor the Elder Emmet & Chambers at Chamber's house in abbey-st which he Farrell & Emmet generally did as Flinn declined acting being engaged in advancing the organization on the Quays & the neighbourhood of Ormond Market where he then resided with his brother. On its being found necessary by the then general executive to have recourse to the forming of an assassination Committee in each of the baronial County & parochial division Farrell the younger Corbett Emmett Jr (Martin Farrell

Information of M[ichael Farrell?] (NAI, Rebellion Papers, 620/11/130/60).

The presence of General Hoche's invasion fleet in Bantry Bay in late December 1796 convinced the United Irishmen and their alarmed government opponents that an Irish Republic was within reach. Robert Emmet's Trinity coterie infiltrated the nominally loyalist college yeomanry corps, while Thomas Addis Emmet joined the Republican Executive Directory in January 1797.

United Irish seals designed by Robert Emmet
(Dúchas/Emmet family and NLI, IR 920041 M11).

Robert Emmet's artistic ability extended to the design of seals and insignia for the Leinster United Irishmen. Possession of such items was a potentially serious offence after the 1795 suppression of the society. An emerald engraved with one of Emmet's designs was sought by the authorities when his brother was arrested at their St Stephen's Green home on the night of 12–13 March 1798.

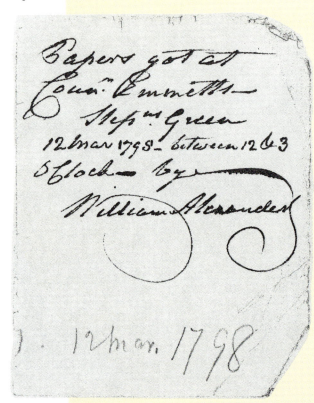

Signet ring with United Irish seal (NMI).

The raid on the Emmet household, St Stephen's Green, 12 March 1798 (NAI, Rebellion Papers, 620/15/2/1).

Magistrate William Alexander led a military raiding party to the Emmet residence on the same night as the bulk of the Provincial Directory of Leinster was arrested in Oliver Bond's house on Bridgefoot Street.

Dr Patrick Duigenan by John Comerford, engraved by James Heath (NLI, EP DUIG-JO (1) 11).

The Right Hon[oura]ble Lord [John] Fitzgibbon by R. Cosway, engraved by F. Bartolozzi (NLI, EP CLAR-JO (1) 1).

Comerford, an Emmet family acquaintance, painted Dr Duigenan, who, with Lord Chancellor Fitzgibbon (Lord Clare), expelled Robert Emmet and eighteen other students from Trinity. This followed the 'Visitation' of 19–22 April when interrogations were held in the Dining Hall, a forum boycotted by Emmet and Farrell.

29

W[illia]m Blacker by Henry Wyndham Phillips, engraved by **William Cook** (NLI, EP BLAC-WI (1) 1).

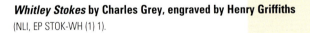

Whitley Stokes by Charles Grey, engraved by Henry Griffiths (NLI, EP STOK-WH (1) 1).

Peter McLoughlin. Pensioner.	John.	Farmer	Dec. 2. 1793. 15 years	C. Mayo
George Keogh. Pensioner.	John.	private Gentleman	Oct. 3. 1796. 13 years	C. Dublin
Bernard Killin. Sizer.	John.	Farmer.	June 13. 1797. 24 years	C. Fermanagh
Edm. Barry — Sizer.	Wm.	Farmer.	May 24. 1796. 19 years	C. Cork.
Thomas Bennett. Sizer.	Thos.	Merchant.	May 24. 1796. 18 years	City Cork.
Robert Emmett. Pensioner.	Robert	Physician	Oct. 7. 1793. 15 years	Dublin.
James Thos. Flinn. Pensioner.	John	Merchant	March 2. 1795. 22 years	Dublin
Mich. Ferrall. Pensioner.	Peter	Farmer.	Nov 3. 1794. 19 years	C. Longford.
... Pennefather Lamphier. Pensioner.	Thomas	private Gentleman	May 6. 1794. 18 years	C. Tipperary.

Trinity Visitation (TCD, MS 1203).

Edward Hudson **by William Cuming, engraved by Timothy S. Engleheart** (NLI, EP HUDS-ED (1) 11).

Antrim Orangeman William Blacker, aged 23 in 1798, denounced Trinity Republicans to Fitzgibbon and Duigenan. Blacker clashed with Dr Whitley Stokes, a lecturer and United Irishman known to the Emmets who was suspended for such improper connections. Edward Hudson was expelled, whereas Thomas Moore was one of at least 30 compromised undergraduates permitted to complete their studies.

31

John Jeffreys Pratt (Marquess of Camden) **by Thomas Lawrence** (NGI, 299).

Mr Secretary Cooke by William Cuming, engraved by James **Heath** (NLI, EP COOK-ED (1) 11).

Lord Viscount Castlereagh, engraved by E. Smith (NLI, EP LOND-RO (5) 1).

Lord Lieutenant Camden (John Jeffreys Pratt), Chief-Secretary Castlereagh (Robert Stewart) and Under-Secretary Edward Cooke responded to the challenge posed by the United Irishmen by declaring martial law. The militarisation of Irish society accelerated after March 1798, and by May the United Irishmen were disposed by the loss of personnel and armaments and the state persecution of innocents to rise without waiting for the French.

To the United Irishmen

My Countrymen and fellow citizens

At a time when you are urged to acts of imprudence by every effort of malice, cunning and tyranny; when illegal and unconstitutional measures are employed to force you into insurrection, and when the members of a most corrupt and infamous Administration are earnestly hoping, and anxiously watching, for the first appearance of rebellion, that they may make it a pretence for destroying some of the most respectable and considerable men in your society, and crushing to the ground the whole body of United Irishmen; I conjure you to guard with the utmost care against being irritated to the degree they wish by their machinations, or inspired as in the way they hope by their real or pretended apprehensions. Is it necessary that I should use any arguments to convince you that the view of the satellites of Government is to provoke you to insurrection before the proper time? Is it not the glaring object of

Address 'To the Dublin United Irishmen' by Robert Emmet
(NAI, Rebellion Papers, 620/15/2/9).

35

Among the papers seized in the Emmet home was a draft address to the Dublin United Irishmen dated 8 March 1798. R.R. Madden ascertained that it was written by Robert Emmet. The document urged restraint in the face of violent provocation and promised ultimate victory. Repeated use of the word 'remember' in the closing paragraphs recalled United Irish slogans 'Remember Armagh' and 'Remember Orr'. Similar language was used by Emmet and Philip Long in 1803.

Kildare House by John Rocque (NLI).

37

Lord Edward Fitzgerald by Hugh Douglas Hamilton (NGI, 195).

Edward Fitzgerald, Kildare's 'Citizen Lord' and former MP, belonged to Ireland's premier titled family and was brother to the progressive Duke of Leinster. His city home, Leinster House, Dublin, was very close to the Emmets', and the two families were well acquainted. By 1797 Fitzgerald, an ex-army officer, was the main military strategist of the United Irishmen. He pioneered urban fighting tactics refined by Emmet, Long and William Dowdall.

The arrest of Lord Edward Fitzgerald (*Young Ireland*, December 1885).

***A view of Moira House* by William Brocas**
(NLI, 2129 (TX) 50).

The betrayal and seizure of Fitzgerald in Thomas Street on 19 May 1798 dealt a serious blow to the uprising planned for the following week. His wife Pamela was staying in Moira House, Usher's Island, a city mansion owned by English Whig leader Earl Moira, who was well disposed toward the United Irishmen.

John Sheares by Adam Buck, engraved by **T.W. Huffam** (NLI, EP SHEA-JO (1) 1).

Henry Sheares by Adam Buck?, engraved by **T.W. Huffam** (NLI, EP SHEA-HE (1) 1).

The Sheares brothers, Cork-born lawyers living in Dublin, assumed senior leadership positions in the United Irishmen after March 1798. John Sheares met Robert Emmet in Trinity and in May 1798 drafted a stirring proclamation emulated by the Dubliner in 1803. The brothers were arrested on 21 May 1798 and executed outside Newgate the following month.

Chapter 3

Rebellion and conspiracy, 1798–1802

The Rebellion of 1798 began with a misfired city plot that ruined any prospect of an unstoppable national wave of popular violence. Elsewhere, partial uprisings met with limited success and engendered an unpredictable and often chaotic showing of arms that took several months and considerable military effort to suppress. The operation of martial law in the capital entailed curfews, patrols and the summary execution of scores of suspected rebels. Many were hanged on Liffey bridges before being dumped into a wastepit in front of the Royal Barracks. United Irishmen fought with tenacity and skill that surprised their opponents and achieved temporary ascendancy in much of Wexford, Wicklow, Kildare, Meath, Carlow, Antrim and Down between late May and mid-June. The arrival of sizeable troop reinforcements from England and Scotland gradually contained the rebellion, but the often difficult campaign of re-conquest cost tens of thousands of lives and millions of pounds. Firepower, training and central command won the day for the government. This also required the granting of a controversially lenient amnesty to secure the demobilisation of the main insurgent armies by mid-July, when several high-profile treason trials were held in Dublin. Significant bodies continued to resist and raid in the inaccessible regions of southern Leinster and east Ulster.

Robert Emmet's role in the Rebellion of 1798 has never been fully documented but was crucial to his subsequent rise through the ranks to a position of leadership. Rebel corps commanded by Francis McMahon and other south city officers known to the Emmets participated in the fighting in the Dublin and Wicklow mountains. Units under elected colonels Southwell McClune of Abbey Street, Felix Rourke of Rathcoole and John Doyle of Plunket Street saw action in Wexford, Kildare and Meath. County and city of Dublin corps were supported by a well-organised coterie of veteran radicals in the capital who had assisted Lord Edward Fitzgerald's Military Committee. For the most part, merchants and professionals with prior military experience, Philip Long, Surgeon Thomas Wright, Hugh O'Hanlon, Charles O'Hara, Patrick Dillon and several other Fitzgerald associates arranged reinforcements, intelligence, finance, supplies and medical treatment for their comrades in the field. They functioned as a substitute leadership and used emissaries in an attempt to coordinate rebel actions in Leinster throughout the summer.

Emmet attended a significant gathering of this group in College Green in late August 1798, when the leaders considered their response to the belated presence of General Jean Humbert's French vanguard in Mayo. The defeat of the main Franco-Irish body at Ballinamuck on 8 September voided any plan agreed in Dublin, but the citymen continued to aid McMahon's group and similar bodies of Wicklowmen under Joseph Holt and Michael Dwyer. Philip Long also extended support to the minority Kildare rebel forces holding out in the Bog of Allen. In late July Emmet liaised with the prominent 'state prisoners' in Kilmainham and Newgate when terms of exile were on offer. This marked him as a reliable and effective operator. He was also clearly militant, given his willingness to join the Executive Directory in January 1799, when all hope of victory seemed forlorn in the short term. Emmet's promotion was sponsored by Wright, Long, O'Hara and others who had been impressed by his conduct during the Rebellion.

The primary task of the new Directory was to prepare the remnants of the United Irishmen to play a constructive role in the event of the French landing in force. The insecure democratic format was jettisoned in favour of a more secretive network of associates who had acquitted themselves well in 1798 and survived its fallout. The rank and file, also trusted veterans, were ordered to remain dormant and to refrain from arms raids. Over one thousand Dublin rebels admitted taking part in the insurrection when seeking conditional pardons, and many more were released from the prison tenders of Dublin Bay in early 1799. Hundreds of Wicklow and Wexford Republicans also moved into the city, finding it impossible to withstand illegal loyalist persecution at home. Securing foreign assistance remained the key to United Irish success, and it was commonly held in Dublin and London that a major invasion would detach Ireland from the British sphere and, quite possibly, presage the fall of the English monarchy.

The government acted on 3 April 1799 by issuing arrest warrants for Emmet and several members of the Directory implicated by Belfast informer James McGucken. Emmet went into hiding in Casino (Milltown), the country seat of his parents on the Dundrum Road, where he had constructed a secret chamber that concealed him from the authorities during raids. He remained a fugitive in Ireland for over a year, during which time he reputedly attended debates in College Green on the proposed Act of Union. The mooted creation of a United Kingdom of Britain and Ireland entailed the abolition of the Ascendancy 'parliament' in Dublin and, while all but inevitable by June 1800, was perceived by the Emmets as a pernicious initiative. Robert Emmet bided his time assisting Wright and Malachy Delaney in writing a manual of paramilitary tactics. A new path was suggested in August 1800 when Edward Carolan arrived from Paris to warn of French concern that the pacific popular response to Union was indicative of its acceptance. Emmet and Delaney were appointed plenipotentiaries and instructed to convince Napoleon Bonaparte that an invasion was still keenly sought.

The backing of the imprisoned pre-Rebellion leadership was desirable, and Emmet travelled to Fort George, Scotland, to confer with his brother Thomas Addis, Thomas Russell, William James MacNeven, Arthur O'Connor and other powerful figures. He met Delaney near Yarmouth, and the pair crossed to Hamburg, where Richard McCormick and other important exiles had settled. General P.F.C. Augereau approved a memorial presented by the delegates and commended it to Bonaparte. They apparently met the most powerful man in the world in January 1801 and were certainly responsible for reassuring him of United Irish commitment to the Republican ideal. While Emmet took lodgings in Paris and prepared documents for the consideration of the French military, the international strategic context suddenly changed in ways that impinged negatively on the interests of the United Irishmen. Preliminary peace negotiations between France and Britain in early 1801 proved successful and paved the way for the signing of the Peace of Amiens in March 1802. While this blow was muted by an expectation of the eventual resumption of war between two diametrically opposed powers, Emmet realised that no invasion fleet could be outfitted while the treaty held. Accordingly, he left Paris and spent much of 1801–2 visiting the major Irish centres on the Continent, including Amsterdam, Brussels, Cadiz and Geneva. Meanwhile, Philip Long, William Dowdall, John Allen and several other post-Rebellion leaders examined the prospects of uniting an Irish insurrection backed by France with a revolutionary effort in England and Scotland. Amiens permitted the deportation to the Continent of many influential 'state prisoners', not least Russell, MacNeven, Neilson and Addis Emmet, who lent their support to the machinations of their successors.

***Robert Emmet* by
Thomas Hickey**
(Kilmainham).

Robert Emmet, a fugitive since April 1798, kept a low profile during the
Rebellion of 1798. He joined a cadre drawn from Lord Edward
Fitzgerald's Military Committee that, in conjunction with a number of
mid-level factions in the south city, functioned as a *de facto* national
leadership throughout the summer. Its surviving members prefigured the
post-Rebellion Executive Directory. This portrait, attributed to the noted
Thomas Hickey, shows Emmet as a young adult and was evidently
painted in or before 1800.

View of the Four Courts by S.F. Brocas (NLI, 519 TB (A)).

Many United Irishmen were hanged on the Liffey bridges and left suspended for days before being thrown into the 'Croppy Hole' (Croppies' Acre) in front of the Royal Barracks, now the National Museum of Ireland, Collins Barracks.

43

R.J.Hamerton.Lith.

Day & Haghe Lith.rs to the Queen.

Joseph Holt by **Robert Jacob Hamerton** (NGI, 10,615).

45

Marquis Cornwallis by H. Walton, engraved by John Ogborne
(NLI, EP CORN-CH (7) II).

Cornwallis succeeded Camden as viceroy in mid-June 1798 and initiated a clemency policy, including amnesty legislation. His arrival coincided with the turning of the military tide against the insurgents arising from the deployment of British reinforcements and the non-appearance of the French. Resistance in the Wicklow and Dublin mountains from insurgents commanded by General Joseph Holt and in other remote sectors of southern Leinster was politically damaging and plagued Cornwallis into the autumn.

Memoire; or, detailed statement of the origin and progress of the Irish Union (Dublin, 1798).

Letter from the state prisoners
(*Saunder's Newsletter*, 27 August 1798).

Cornwallis approved a pact with the state prisoners in August 1798 whereby they were excused trial for high treason if they went into exile. Robert Emmet was involved in negotiations with the senior United Irishmen detained in Kilmainham, Newgate and the Bridewell. A small minority including Roger O'Connor and William Dowdall opposed the deal even if the lives of Oliver Bond and Samuel Neilson would be preserved. Addis Emmet, MacNeven and Arthur O'Connor, in accordance with terms agreed with Cornwallis, provided government with limited and disingenuous details of their contact with the French. All three signed a letter of protest when their position was misrepresented in the press by the Castle.

Roger O'Connor by **Adam Buck** (NLI, EP OCON-RO (2) 1).

The French in Killala Bay (1798), **artist unknown** (NGI, 1772).

Barth[olome]w Teeling, **engraved by James Henry Lynch** (NLI, EP TEEL-BA (1) 1).

The landing near Killala, Mayo, of a small French force under General Jean Joseph Humbert in late August 1798 briefly transformed the Rebellion in Connacht. Emmet attended a meeting of United Irish officers in College Green, Dublin, which decided to conserve the organisation's resources until a major invasion occurred. Bartholomew Teeling was executed after capture, notwithstanding his French army commission. Robert Emmet was a close associate of Teeling's younger brother George and evidently wrote *Arbour Hill* ('No rising column marks the spot') to commemorate Teeling's burial in Croppies' Acre. The Rebellion ground to a halt in late autumn with the exception of small bands such as those led by Michael Dwyer and John Mernagh in Wicklow, Thomas Archer in Antrim, James Corcoran in Wexford and John Doorley in Kildare.

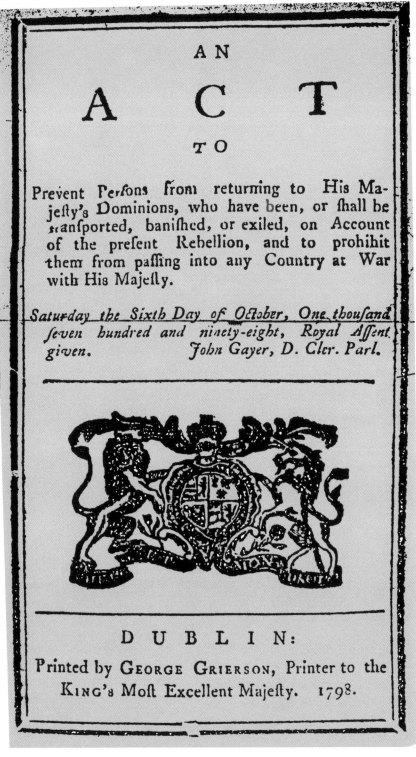

The Banishment Act (private collection).

Signatories of the 'Kilmainham pact' and other political prisoners were deported to Fort George, Scotland, in the spring of 1799. Those interned and banished from Ireland and Britain were threatened with execution if they returned without permission.

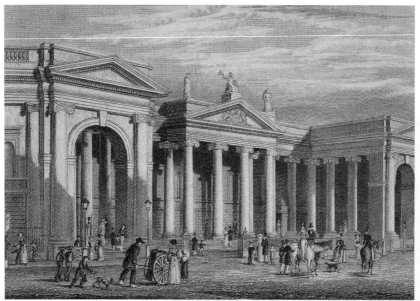

Bank of Ireland by George Petrie, engraved by Benjamin Winkles (NGI, 11,785).

Earl of Granard (NLI, Barrington).

Robert Holmes, engraved by Henry Griffiths (NLI, EP HOLM-RO (2) 1).

Proposals to create a United Kingdom of Great Britain and Ireland divided the political establishment in Dublin. The Emmets were in contact with the Earl of Granard and liberal gentry who feared that the abolition of the national forum was a retrograde step. Robert Holmes, a barrister and yeoman shown here in later life, was chastised for publishing anti-Union propaganda, as was his secret fiancée, Mary Anne Emmet. Robert Emmet also vehemently opposed Union and reputedly attended debates on the bill. This was complicated by an attempt to arrest him at Casino, Milltown, in April 1799 for membership of the United Irish Directory. The Irish Parliament was dissolved on 1 January 1801, and the Bank of Ireland, in which Dr Robert Emmet was a major investor, obtained the Parliament buildings.

Duelling pistols of the Emmet family (Dúchas/Emmet family).

Emmet's wallet (NMI).

Emmet left Dublin in August 1800 and conferred in secret with the state prisoners interned in Fort George, Scotland. John Patten, his cousin, had previously couriered these pistols to the fortress for an intended duel between Thomas Addis Emmet and Arthur O'Connor but the negotiating skills of Robert Emmet secured its cancellation.

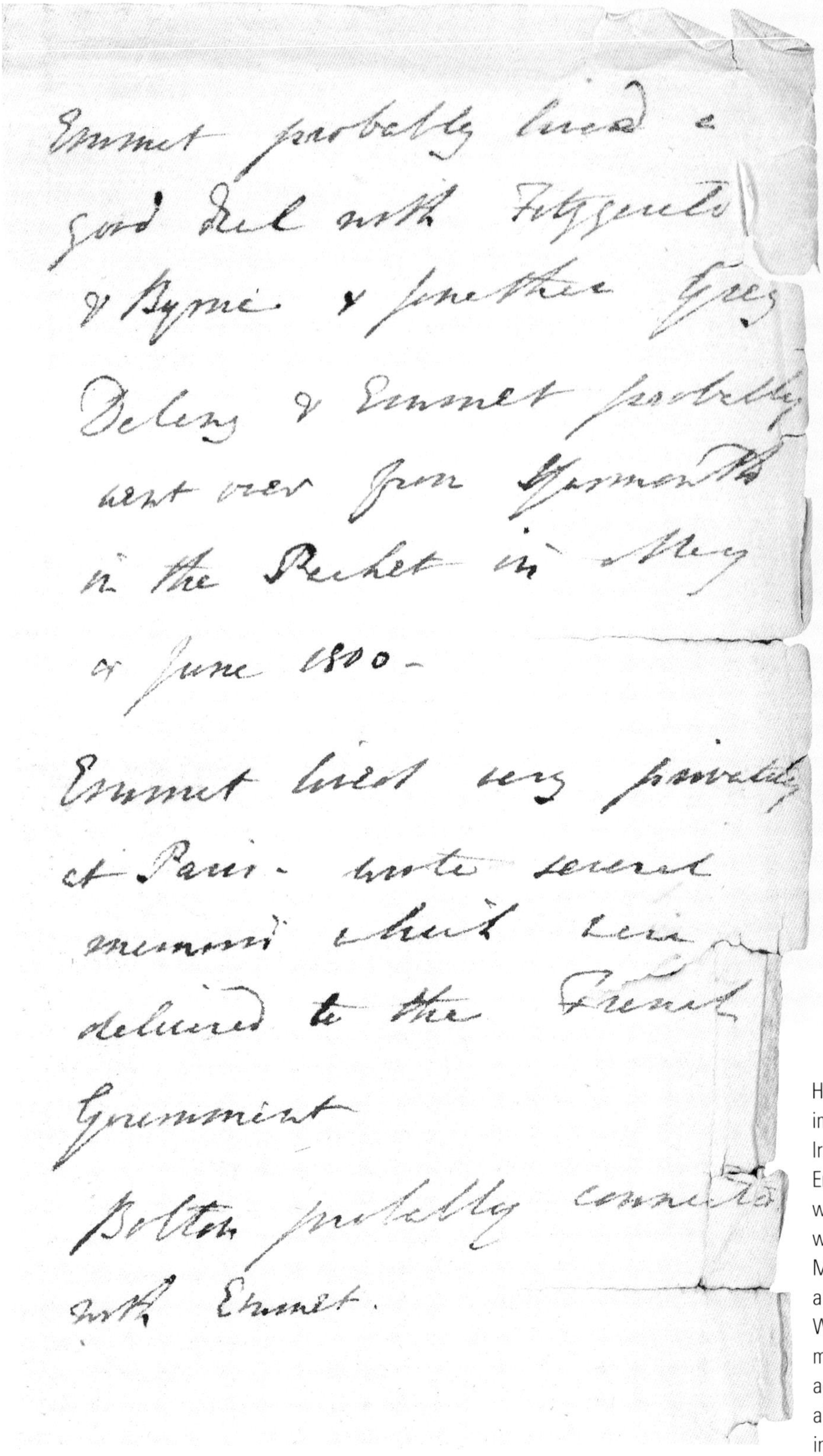

Emmet probably lived a
good deal with Fitzgerald
& Byrne & another Greg

Delany & Emmet probably
went over from Yarmouth
in the Packet in May
or June 1800 –

Emmet lived very privately
at Paris – wrote several
memoirs which were
delivered to the French
Government

Bolton probably connected
with Emmet.

Information of 'Fullar' (NAI, Rebellion Papers, 620/11/130/43).

Having obtained the support of the imprisoned former leadership of the United Irishmen for the new military strategy, Emmet crossed from Yarmouth to Hamburg with Malachy Delaney. They spent time with ex-Directory member Richard McCormick, as well as Edward Fitzgerald and Garret Byrne, former commanders of Wexford and Wicklow rebels. Their movements were monitored by double agent Samuel Turner and one 'Fullar', although their full import was only realised in retrospect.

Edward Fitzgerald of Newpark, Co. Wexford by **Thomas Nugent, engraved by W.T. Annis** (NGI, 10,211).

Billy [recte Garret] Byrne of Ballymanus
(Presidential Collection, Áras an Uachtaráin).

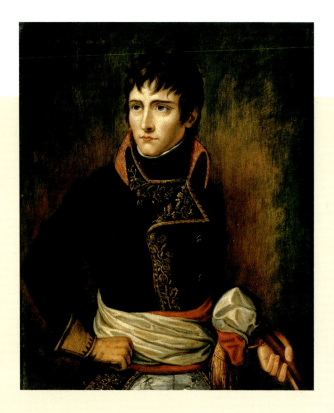

Bonaparte as a General of the Army of the Revolution, artist unknown (NGI, 1189).

General [P.F.C.] Augereau, the victor of Castilione (NLI, J 94405).
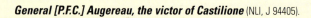

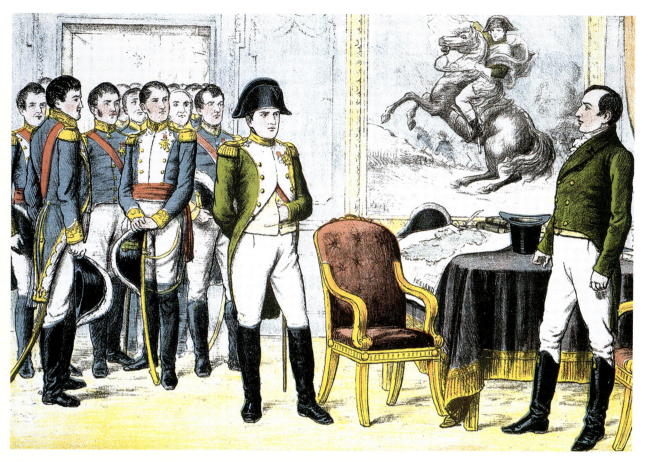

Emmet's interview with Napoleon by **J.D. Reigh** (*Shamrock*, December 1895).

Portrait of Tallyrand (NLI, J 94405 A).

The memorial presented by Emmet and Delaney to General P.F.C. Augereau was endorsed by Bonaparte in January 1801. Emmet informed Miles Byrne of his subsequent interviews in Paris with the First Consul and Foreign Minister, Charles-Maurice de Tallyrand.

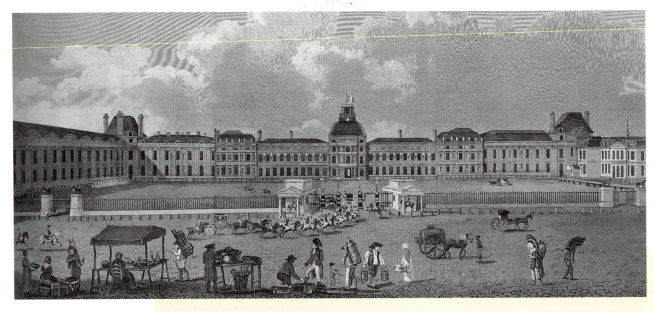

Palace of the Tuileries facing La Place Du Carrousel, **engraved by Sparrow** (NLI, J 9140).

Entrance to Les Champs Elysees and La Place de la Concorde (NLI, J 9140).

57

Robert Fulton Esqr. **by R. West, engraved by W.S. Lenry** (Emmet, *Memoir*).

When living in Paris in 1801–2 Emmet befriended the American inventor Robert Fulton, who deepened Emmet's interest in military technology. Emmet and Delaney remained in close contact with the United Irish communities on the Continent after the March 1802 Peace of Amiens temporarily removed the French from Ireland's revolutionary equation.

Arthur O'Connor. General de Division by J. Godefroy, engraved by François P.S. Gérard (NLI, EP OCON-AR (4) 1).

Thomas Addis Emmet, **artist unknown** (NGI, 3867).

The gradual release of the Fort George internees in late 1802 enabled
the reunion of Robert and Thomas Addis Emmet in Amsterdam. It also
revived tension between the Emmet brothers and Arthur O'Connor's
minority clique, which favoured a much stronger French invasion force
than that envisaged in Dublin after 1798.

Chapter 4

The Rising of 1803

Emmet returned to Ireland in October 1802, when it was hoped that war would be resumed by Britain and France within months. It was imperative to assess the capacity of the United Irishmen to play their part in a struggle that threatened to engulf both islands of the new United Kingdom. Emmet conferred with John Keogh and other longstanding leaders of means whose financial and moral support was deemed important to reviving Republican fortunes. Neilson paid a fleeting visit to Ireland during the early winter months and met Emmet amid great secrecy in Milltown. The Belfastman travelled on to New York with the intention of founding a radical newspaper but liaised before his departure with members of the Teeling, Simms, O'Hara and Palmer families, who featured prominently in the United Irish underground. He also availed of the conspiratorial acumen of Antrim's James Hope, whom Emmet quickly took into his confidence regarding the positive news from France. Hope, Miles Byrne and Arthur Devlin began to agitate in the displaced communities of Wexford and Wicklow rebels who lived in the capital, as well as the manufacturing workers of the south city, where hundreds of 1798 veterans lived. These men, along with columns of handpicked associates from the surrounding counties, were to lead a *coup d'état* in the capital when the French landed. As war neared, Michael Quigley and Bryan McDermott returned illegally from France to establish contact with the dormant Kildare networks. Their arrival on 5 March 1803 heralded a discrete influx of senior figures, not least Thomas Russell and William Hamilton. Rebellion hero Thomas Cloney moved back from Liverpool, and steps were taken to build up a network of arsenals and safe houses for the use of the leadership and its assistants.

The death of Dr Robert Emmet on 9 December 1802, following closely upon a raid on his Milltown residence, placed his eponymous son in command of £2000 to invest in the planned revolution. Philip Long and well-placed sympathisers furnished greater sums to lease and commission premises where weaponry was stockpiled and manufactured. The main depot was on Marshal Lane South, to the rear of Thomas Street's White Bull Inn, and up to nine more buildings had been obtained by the summer of 1803. A depot at 26 Patrick Street, where signal and explosive rockets were assembled, was devastated by an accidental explosion on 16 July. Two men were mortally wounded, and the incident threatened to expose the full range of United Irish preparations. Emmet, Dowdall, Allen, Long and Russell decided to mount a partial uprising on the east coast while the element of confusion, if not surprise, gave them an advantage over the authorities. They reasoned that the civil and military establishment remained vulnerable and, if removed by an insurrection in the metropolis, could not be restored if a national uprising ensued in support of the first decapitating blow. Moreover, a major effort by the United Irishmen was deemed likely to encourage the French to send immediately the reinforcements necessary to guarantee Irish independence from British counter-attack. The date was fixed for 23 July, and senior emissaries were dispatched from Dublin to apprise provincial adherents.

Russell found on returning to Antrim and Down that a hitherto militant sector was reluctant to fight if neither the French nor significant supplies of firearms were provided. Hope and Hamilton experienced similar setbacks in Fermanagh, Cavan, Monaghan and other counties that had previously undertaken to form the first wave of uprisings. The full extent of this reserve was not appreciated in the capital on the morning of 23 July, when Emmet's agents rode into County Dublin, Kildare and Wicklow to warn their allies to hold themselves in readiness. There were also expectations of armed actions by Wexford and Meath insurgents whose leaders were in regular contact with the conspirators. Thousands of Kildare and County Dublin rebels were required to back their comrades in the south city by massing on Thomas Street at 6.00pm, where final instructions and the weaponry needed to strike at 9.00pm would be issued. The main force, however, consisted of elite and veteran United Irishmen who formed up, fully armed and tasked, in a number of strategic locations around the capital. They were to spearhead the assaults on key installations, reinforced by the influx of supporters from the surrounding countryside. All major road routes were to be cut in the suburbs to isolate the Executive further when three signal rockets alerted cadres in Islandbridge, Sandymount, Phibsborough, Lucan, Rathfarnham and elsewhere to initiate coordinated armed actions.

A series of misunderstandings between Dublin Castle and army headquarters ensured that the authorities, though forewarned of the probability of unrest, were unprepared to respond to its manifestation. The Privy Council was not summoned; the Lord Lieutenant remained in the Phoenix Park; and the Commander-in-Chief of the army failed to implement countermeasures. Unaware of such unanticipated advantages, Emmet and his advisors became gravely concerned by disparate acts of ill discipline among their followers that threatened the cohesion of their plans. Negative reports from certain sectors and the breakdown of communications with others, not least Wicklow and Wexford, led to the abandonment of several objectives. Matters came to a head when Kildare officers realised that promised firearms were not available, and many hundreds of their adherents left for home before 6.00pm. When shooting incidents and arms raids suggested the imminent implosion of the conspiracy, Emmet concentrated on storming the Castle. This, however, became impractical when the man entrusted with gathering the necessary coaches neglected his orders.

Faced with an anarchic and seemingly doomed situation, Emmet decided to countermand the rising and launched a solitary rocket to signal cancellation. The hundreds who gathered around the city melted away, while the special squads in Wood Quay, Ship Street, Thomas Court and elsewhere stood down. On reading extracts from the Proclamation of the Provisional Government, a gesture of defiance that enabled his already compromised followers to claim political motivation for their deeds, Emmet led a much reduced column of 200 men toward the Castle with a view to leading them out of the city to the Dublin Mountains. Any chance of this feint becoming an opportunist attack on the Executive was discarded when the chance entanglement of Lord Kilwarden's carriage with the rear of the Thomas Street force exposed Emmet's lack of authority. Emmet and most of the senior leadership promptly left for Rathfarnham.

Several mid-level commanders who either misunderstood the earlier rocket signal or wished to engage the garrison regardless of orders fought a series of skirmishes between 9.45pm and 11.00pm with soldiers of the 21st Regiment. Scores of casualties were endured and inflicted in the Coombe and the backstreets of the south city. In each case the outnumbered military withdrew to barracks, leaving their opponents on the streets. By the time a coordinated response to the crisis was organised, the vast majority of participants had safely dispersed. This revealed something of the scope of a full-blown surprise attack envisaged by Emmet's leadership and marked one of the few occasions in which irregulars confronted regular soldiers on the streets of the Irish capital.

Robert Emmet Esqr **by James Petrie, engraved by James Heath** (NLI, PD EMME-RO (2) II).

John Keogh **by John Comerford**
(NGI, 7200).

Robert Emmet returned to Dublin in October 1802 and canvassed support for a United Irish uprising to coincide with a French invasion. John Keogh, an early and wealthy Republican, entertained Emmet in Mount Jerome (Harold's Cross) and heard him declare that nineteen counties would participate.

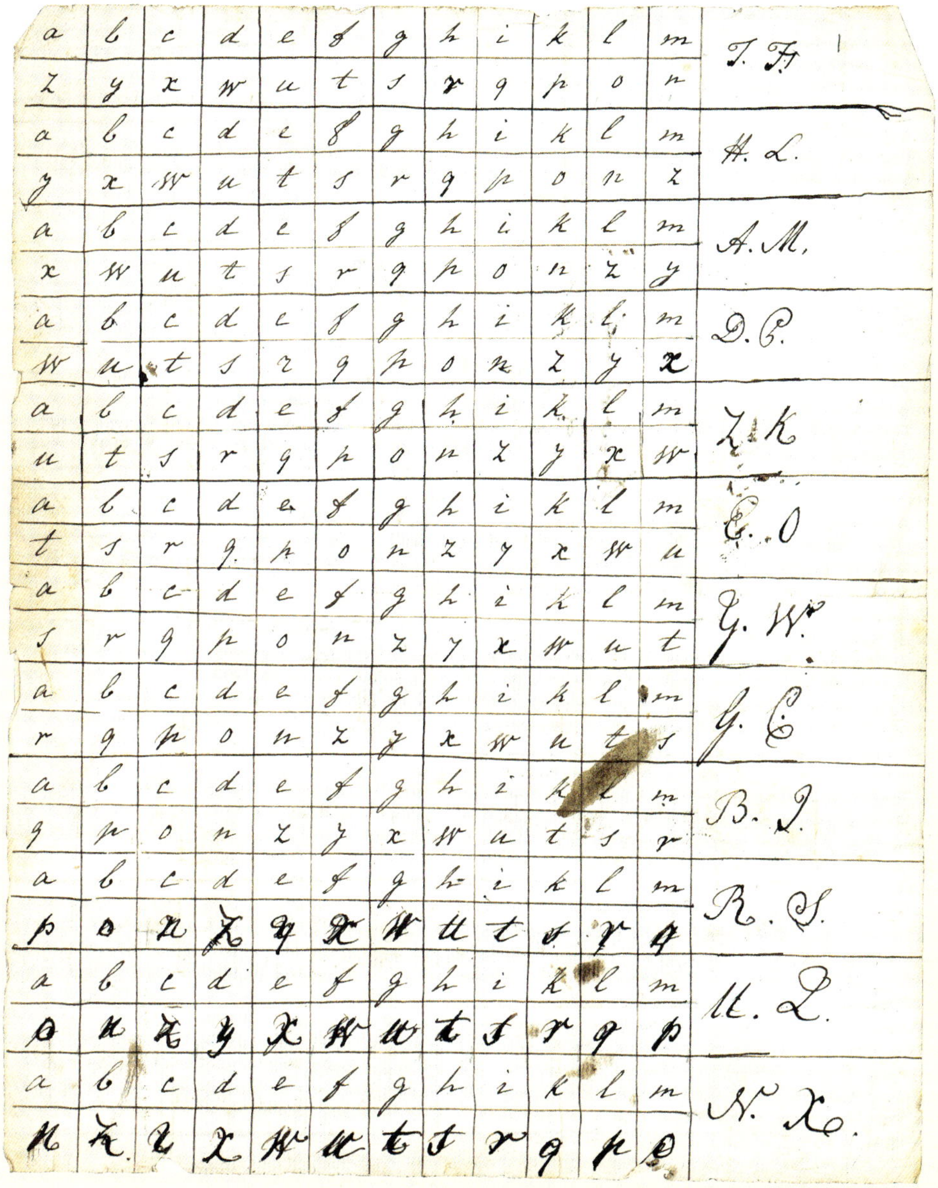

William Dowdall's code sheet
(NAI, Rebellion Papers,
620/12/143/58).

Robert Emmet, William Dowdall, Philip Long and John Allen, the core
Dublin leadership of the Rising of 1803, used aliases, Masonic
recognition signals, invisible ink, ciphers and code phrases to disguise
their identities and communications from hostile parties. Emmet
reputedly used dice when dealing with emissaries and was successful
in shielding his intentions from the Castle.

Felix Rourke by James Petrie (NLI, Elmes, 176).

Thomas Russell (*Walker's Hibernian Magazine*, 1803).

Edward Hay, Esqr. Secretary to the Irish Catholic Committee (NLI, EP HAY-ED (1) 1).

Felix Rourke of Rathcoole, Co. Dublin, an important United Irish organiser and colonel of insurgents in 1798, added his considerable reputation to the conspiracy in early 1803. His pre-Rebellion associate Edward Farrell was also reactivated. Thomas Russell followed Kildare exiles Michael Quigley of Rathcoffey and Bryan McDermott of Hodgestown back from France to assist Emmet. Wexford leaders Edward Hay of Ballinkeele and Robert Carty of Birchgrove, though privy to their plans, were non-committal.

Miles Byrne by Mrs Byrne (Whelan, *Fellowship of freedom*).

James Hope, engraved by T.W. Huffam (NLI, EP HOP-JA 1).

Miles Byrne of Monaseed organised Wexford residents of Dublin's south city in 1802–3. James Hope of Templepatrick, a highly experienced agitator, prepared the Coombe district to fight again and ventured into Wicklow to liaise with Michael Dwyer's guerrilla faction.

Sarah Curran's spinet (Dúchas/Emmet family).

Sarah Curran's music book (NLI, MS 10,650).

Robert Emmet's romantic attachment to Sarah Curran of The Priory, Rathfarnham, sister of his Trinity friend Richard Curran and daughter of United Irish lawyer John Philpot Curran, deepened on his return to Ireland. They became secretly engaged before July 1803 and exchanged correspondence indicating Curran's awareness of Emmet's seditious activities.

Embroidered map of Ireland by Sarah Curran, 1802 (NLI, Acc 5079).

Michael Dwyer **by James Petrie** (NGI, 11,182).

Dwyer, a United Irish hero figure, met Emmet in Rathfarnham in April
1803 and agreed to reinforce a city revolt. The Wicklowman was drawn in
Kilmainham after December 1803 by James Petrie.

Two views of Emmet's house, Butterfield Lane
(Emmet, *Memoir*, and *Weekly Freeman*, 10 December 1910).

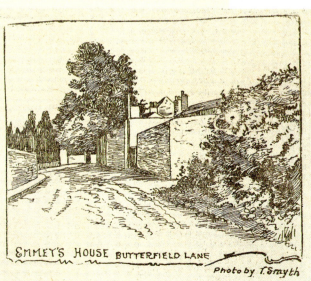

Emmet leased a house in Butterfield Lane, Rathfarnham, where he planned the Rising with senior associates and briefed rural emissaries. Anne Devlin, confidante and messenger, played the role of housekeeper to present an air of normality. Anne Palmer's house in Harold's Cross, where Emmet called himself 'Hewitt', was also used, as were basement rooms in Capel Street, Dublin.

70

The Volunteers of the City and County of Dublin, as they met on College Green (NLI, PD HP (1779) 1).

The revocation of martial law in 1802 encouraged Dublin Republicans to recommence harassing the loyalist community and celebrating Bastille Day (14 July) with huge bonfires. Clashes occurred near Kevin Street fountain and King William's equestrian statue at College Green.

Parliament House, Dublin by **William Brocas** (NLI, BR 1963 TX (4A)).

Robert Emmet and Michael Dwyer in Marshalsea Lane depot, 1803 (*Shamrock*, December 1896).

73

St Catharine's [sic] Church, Thomas Street, Dublin by **James Malton** (NLI, PD 3181 TX 117).

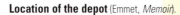

Location of the depot (Emmet, *Memoir*).

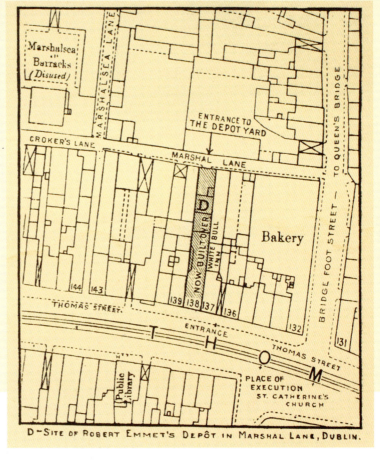

'Emmet's chair' (The Brazen Head).

The conspirators leased a malt store in Marshal Lane South (see pages 72–3) , to the rear of Thomas Street, where they sited the largest of an estimated ten arsenals. Michael Quigley ran the central depot, in which Emmet kept personal effects and occasionally met confederates. Over 5000 pikes, 140lbs of gunpowder and 300 improvised grenades were stored behind false partition walls.

DUBLIN, JULY 19.

Sunday morning laſt, about four o'cook, two men, one of them carrying a caſk on his ſhoulder, were ſtopped by two watchmen, (according to their uſual orders) near Patrick-ſtreet and the Poddle; the watch required that it ſhould be brought to the watch-houſe, to be examined by a peace officer. Theſe men uſed ſome equivocating expreſſions, and obſerved that if the watchmen would go a few paces with them, they ſhould be ſatisfied as to the contents of the caſk. They brought them accordingly to the door of one Palmer, a retailer of ſpirits, the corner of New-row on the Poddle, at whoſe door they rapped, and not being immediately anſwered, they flung ſome gravel at the windows, to haſten, it is ſuppoſed, attention to their application. While this was going on, both the fellows, watching opportunity, ran away, dropping the caſk behind them on the ground. They were purſued by two watchmen as far as Kevin-ſtreet, (leaving the caſk in care of another) but there a poſſe collected to oppoſe them, and protect the runaways; the watch were of courſe obliged to retreat. The caſk being ſomewhat broke on falling to the ground, there fell out of it ſome flints and iron rings, and on ſearching, it was found to contain powder and ball cartridges made up in parcels of 24 rounds, flints, &c.

The Watchmen proceeded to take it to the watch-houſe; but before they could get half-way, a numerous aſſemblage of perſons from Patrick-ſtreet, and Kevin-ſtreet, to the number of at leaſt 200, ſome of them well dreſſed, and armed with guns and blunderbuſſes, appeared, fired ſome ſhots, and reſcued the caſk from the watchmen. The latter were obliged to fly in conſequence of the attack of ſuch a numerous body; but it is lamented, that they could not get aſſiſtance from the military who were near the place, at a guard-houſe, on the Comb, otherwiſe the ammunition caſk would have been ſecured, and ſome of thoſe daring deſperadoes. The peace officer, Mr. Wilſon, came ſhortly afterwards to the place with a party of petty conſtables; but all the ruffians had diſappeared.

A fire having happened at a houſe in Patrick-ſtreet, on Saturday evening, and it being mentioned to Mr. Wilſon that an exploſion of gunpowder was heard at it, he conceived it might have been from this place that came, which was in the caſk ſtopped on Sunday morning; he went to the ſpot, on Sunday night, where the fire had happened, and on making a very minute ſearch, he found there, and in an adjoining houſe, a machine for making powder, with an apparatus, ſome ſalt-petre prepared for the manufacture, and up a chimney ſome bayonets that had been fixed on poles, and a number of handles provided for others, with a quantity of balls, all of which were ſeized, and brought to the Superintendant Magiſtrate's; and this circumſtance proved that it was from that place the caſk with the ammunition came on Sunday morning, in order to have it ſecreted. At the fire which took place, as before mentioned, on Saturday night, in Patrick-ſtreet, two men were ſo much burned, that they were brought to Stevens's hoſpital. This was an occurrence neceſſarily to be enquired into, and on the Superintendant Magiſtrate having the affair inveſtigated on Monday morning, it was found one of the wretched men had died in the hoſpital.

The other much burned was taken into cuſtody, and examined ſtrictly by the Superintendant Magiſtrate; but the priſoner, who ſays his name is Pat. Bourne, would not acknowledge to have been concerned in making gunpowder. He has however been committed to gaol, under the care of a ſurgeon. He ſays he is not long in Dublin, ſince he came from ſea; had entered in the year 79, and was for years on board the Leviathan, of 74 guns; is a native of Shillelagh, in the county of Wexford. In the ſearch of the houſe in Patrick-ſtreet, a receipt was found for the purchaſe of the powder-machine from Mr. O'Reilly, of Church ſtreet; it coſt five guineas, and the name of the perſon ſtated to have bought it, is Mackintoſh. Mr. O'Reilly was brought before the Superintendant Magiſtrate, and examined as to the tranſaction; as was alſo Palmer, to the door of whoſe houſe the caſk with amunition was brought at the time it was ſeized by the watch. The Peace-officers and watchmen have been moſt indefatigable in this affair, and deſerve the ſtrongeſt acknowledgments of applauſe from the public. The man who died of the exploſion at the fire, was of the name, it is ſaid, of Keenan; from further inveſtigations which are to take place of this very extraordinary affair, it will no doubt appear that this has been a very fortunate diſcovery.

The Patrick Street explosion (*Freeman's Journal*, 19 July 1803).

The explosion of powder being prepared to prime rockets on 16 July 1803 mortally wounded two of Emmet's men and destroyed John McIntosh's Patrick Street workshop. McIntosh's surviving team fought off the firemen until the paraphernalia of illegal arms manufacture was dispersed to safe houses. Government suspicions were played down in the press, but Emmet, meeting United Irish leaders in Kilmacud that night, surmised that the vital secret of the depots had been compromised. The resultant decision to rise without the French ensured that the scale of fighting envisaged in Emmet's military writings did not occur.

Military Regulations of the Council of War

Found this paper in
the Depot 24th July 1803

1 Every Officer shall throw under them on
the duty within it is necessary for them to know — once a week
& make a return of those who have distinguished
themselves in that & their General conduct — These
shall be put on the list of Candidates for Promotion
& the vacancies that occur filled up — out of them it

2 No person but a Soldier shall be admitted within the encamp-
-ment A Place shall be fixed on to which the Camp is
least exposed for Strangers No Captain is to suffer
more than ⅙th of his Company at a time to go to it

3 Before any Soldier is enrolled the Articles of War — & an
Abstract of such Military Regulations as concern him
he shall then take the Oath subjoined — These shall also
be read
An Officer shall read to him

4 Once in every Week at the head of the Battalion.
& any soldier that refuses to obey them shall have
permission to quit the ranks —

5 — The Major

Moved by

'Military regulations of the Council of War' (NAI, Rebellion Papers, 620/12/155/2).

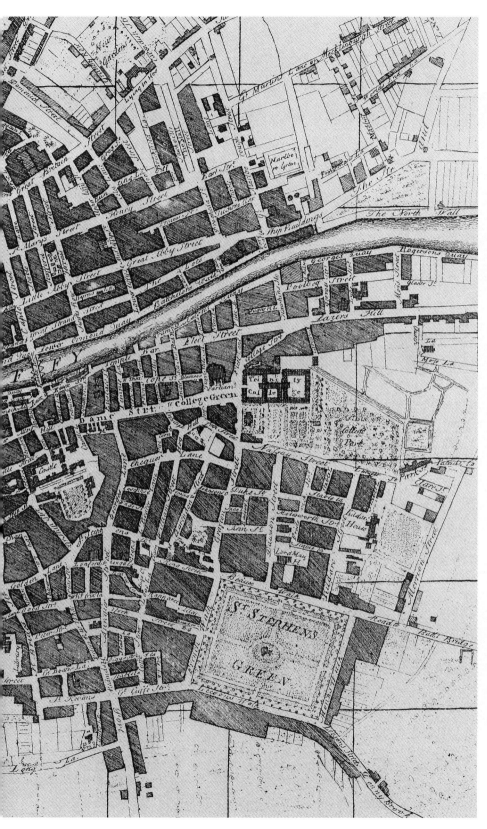

Peter Wilson's map of Dublin
(private collection).

79

Wilson's map of Dublin shows the strategic importance of the sector of the south city separating Kilmainham from Dublin Castle. Smithfield, north of the Liffey, contained munitions depots and rebel cadres, but they, and their comrades who gathered at Broadstone and elsewhere, were not committed to the fighting.

Lieutenant General Henry Edward Fox by J.W. Chandler.

Under-Secretary Alexander Marsden.

Lord Lieutenant Philip York (Earl Hardwicke).

General Fox, newly appointed and disdainful of civilian administrators, was not well briefed by Dublin Castle on the deteriorating security situation on 23 July 1803. Chief-Secretary William Wickham was in England, and Under-Secretary Alexander Marsden proved incapable of explaining the nature of the unrest anticipated. While Lord Lieutenant Hardwicke remained in the Phoenix Park, Fox assumed in army headquarters (Kilmainham) that the civilian yeomanry had been mobilised. Marsden, in the Castle, wrongly believed that Fox had ordered troops onto the streets. In fact, no public buildings were protected, and neither the yeomanry nor the army received orders to patrol.

A view of the Pigeon House, Dublin **by William Sadler** (NGI, 632).

The Pigeon House, fortified in 1798, was an objective of the 1803
conspirators and reconnoitred by their agents. An arms dump was
established in Irishtown under the control of Thomas Brannigan.

Old Soldiers Hospital, Kilmainham, Dublin by James Malton (NLI, PD 3181 TX 97).

Dublin's inner suburb of Kilmainham, site of the county prison and court, also contained General Fox's headquarters in the Royal Hospital. These lay across the Liffey from Islandbridge artillery barracks and the Phoenix Park Magazine, intended targets of the United Irishmen.

The gravest threat to the city insurgents was posed by the 2100 soldiers of the 32nd and 38th Regiments housed in the Royal Barracks and the 600 men of the 62nd Regiment in the Custom House Barracks on the corner of Essex and Parliament streets. Emmet planned to defend the approaches from the Royal Barracks to the south city using barricades defended by elevated marksmen, grenadiers and explosive devices known as 'infernals'. This would enable the rebels to muster in strength on Thomas Street, the main thoroughfare separating army headquarters from the Castle. The Custom House Barracks and more distant Cork Street Barracks, home to the 21st Regiment, were both considered for first-wave assaults.

Facing page
Barracks, Dublin by James Malton (NLI, PD 3181 TX 147).

The Custom House, Dublin by Charles Brooking, engraved by **John Bowles** (NGI, 10,015 (14)).

View of Dublin from the Magazine, Phoenix Park by James **Malton** (NLI, PD 3181 TX 151).

Hardwicke, after a short conference with Fox and Marsden in the Castle in the early afternoon of 23 July, spent the rest of the day in his country residence. His bodyguard was not increased until after the danger had subsided, and there is little doubt but that he would have been killed or captured had Emmet persevered with plans to attack the Viceregal

The Mansion House, Lord Mayor's residence, Dublin by **Charles Brooking, engraved by John Bowles** (NGI, 10,015 (8)).

Henry Howley by **James Petrie** (NLI, EP HOWL-HE (1)).

An arms raid on the Mansion House in the early evening was one of numerous incidents that confirmed warnings of United Irish intentions. The wounding of two Palmerstown magistrates, Edward Clarke and Richard Willcocks, on Arran Quay, and separate attacks on their city colleagues Edward Wilson, Oliver Carleton and Frederick Darley, convinced Marsden that the army was not positioned to pre-empt the emergency. Oblivious to this opportunity, Emmet grew despondent at the ill discipline of a small section of his followers and the refusal of several Kildare and County Dublin units to fight without the firearms they had been promised. He scaled down the plans for the Rising and all but abandoned it when Henry Howley shot Colonel Lyde Brown on Bridgefoot Street instead of procuring carriages required to assault the Castle.

Sir

It is with heartfelt anxiety and concern that I have to acquaint you of my being informed a few days agoe that the disaffected party in this city aided by thousands from different parts of the country intended a Rising upon the very first news they would receive of the french landing in either this Country or England, though the above information made no very serious Impression at the time upon my mind yet I intended acquainting Mr Wickham of it the moment of his arrival which I hoped would have been ere now it is not in the power of Language to convey to you sir an Idea of my feelings and distress of mind at being this moment informed by the same person (who is as Loyal a subject as any the King has but not thought so by the deluded wretches above alluded to) that there is the most Vigorous preparations making for an attack upon the Kings troops this very night I am also told by the same person that there are warehouses full of Pikes fire arms and Ammunition concealed in this city but exactly where I could not learn would to Heaven I could and thereby stop the dreadfule consequences in the Bud — the miscreants intend attacking the Garrison at the Pidgeon House the Castle and in short every place of defence — I hope and trust in the Almighty god. that such a thing may never be attempted but that it is in contemplation I have no more doubt of than I have of my existence. — though I detest the appellation of an Informer yet as a Loyal subject of the best of Kings I wd deem myself very culpable indeed if I did not thus apprise his Majesties Govern. of such a dreadfule conspiracy — any further Intelligence I can procure shall be immediately made known to you — being fully persuaded you will order the necessary precautions to be adopted —

Dublin Saturday 4 OClock —
July 23rd 1803 —

A. Marsden Esqr. & & & .

I Have the Honor to be Sir —
a lover of My King and country
and your Humble Servt —
a Loyal Irishman

'A loyal Irishman' to Marsden (NAI, Rebellion Papers, 620/65/194).

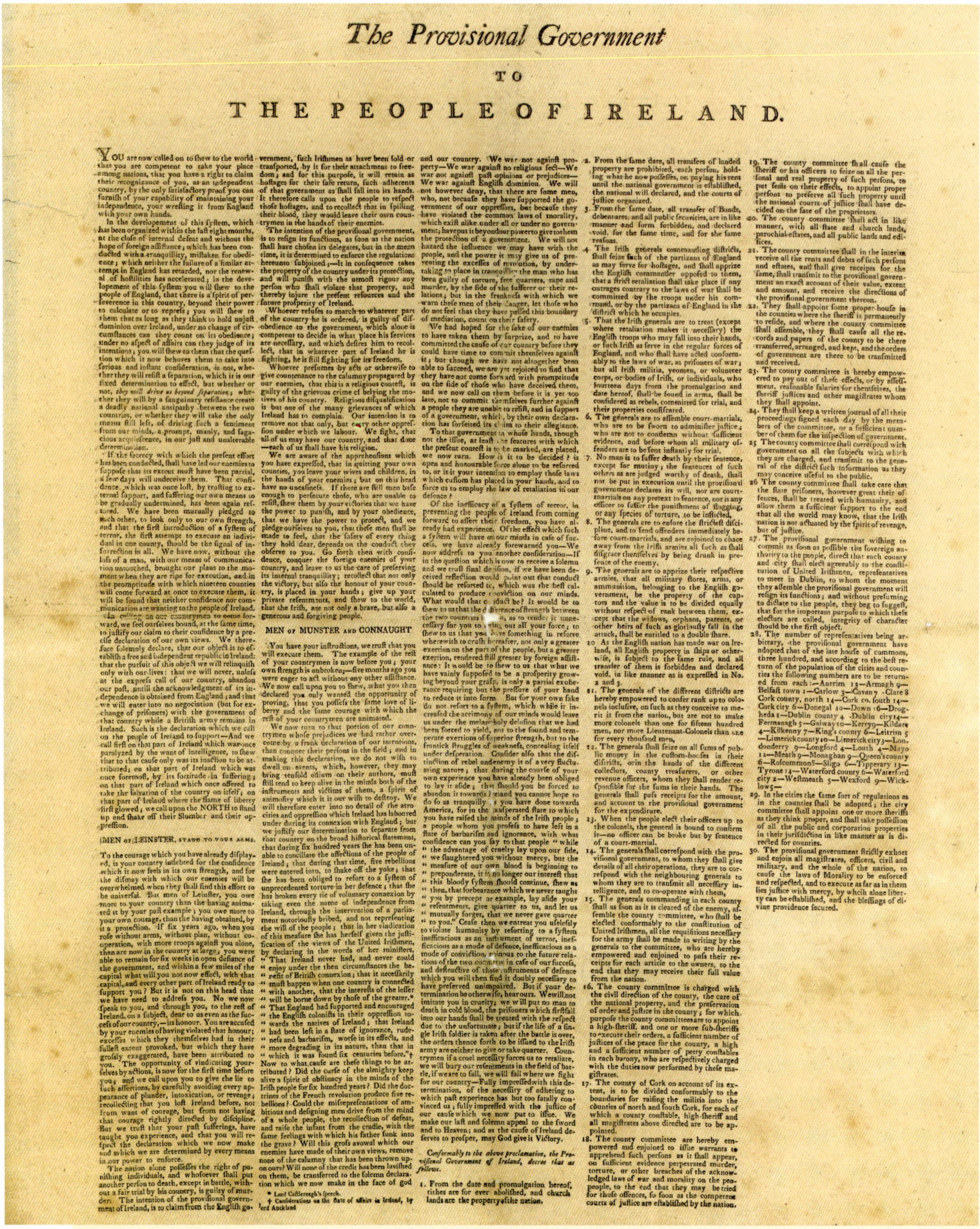

The Provisional Government

TO

THE PEOPLE OF IRELAND.

You are now called on to shew to the world that you are competent to take your place among nations, that you have a right to claim their recognizance of you, as an independent country, by the only satisfactory proof you can furnish of your capability of maintaining your independence, your wresting it from England with your own hands.

In the developement of this system, which has been organized within the last eight months, at the close of internal defeat and without the hope of foreign assistance; which has been conducted with a tranquillity, mistaken for obedience; which neither the failure of a similar attempt in England has retarded, nor the renewal of hostilities has accelerated; in the developement of this system you will shew to the people of England, that there is a spirit of perseverence in this country, beyond their power to calculate or to repress; you will shew to them that as long as they think to hold unjust dominion over Ireland, under no change of circumstances can they count on its obedience; under no aspect of affairs can they judge of its intentions; you will shew to them that the question which it now behoves them to take into serious and instant consideration, is not, whether they will resist a separation, which it is our fixed determination to effect, but whether or not, *they will drive us beyond separation*; whether they will by a sanguinary resistance create a deadly national antipathy between the two countries, or whether they will take the only means still left, of driving such a sentiment from our minds, a prompt, manly, and sagacious acquiescence, in our just and unalterable determination.

If the secrecy with which the present effort has been conducted, shall have led our enemies to suppose that its extent must have been partial, a few days will undeceive them. That confidence, which was once lost, by trusting to external support, and suffering our own means to be gradually undermined, has been again restored. We have been mutually pledged to each other, to look only to our own strength, and that the first introduction of a system of terror, the first attempt to execute an individual in one county, should be the signal of insurrection in all. We have now, without the loss of a man, with our means of communication untouched, brought our plans to the moment when they are ripe for execution, and in the promptitude with which nineteen counties will come forward at once to execute them, it will be found that neither confidence nor communication are wanting to the people of Ireland.

In calling on our countrymen to come forward, we feel ourselves bound, at the same time, to justify our claim to their confidence by a precise declaration of our own views. We therefore solemnly declare, that our object is to establish a free and independent republic in Ireland: that the pursuit of this object we will relinquish only with our lives: that we will never, unless at the express call of our country, abandon our post, untill the acknowledgment of its independence is obtained from England; and that we will enter into no negociation (but for exchange of prisoners) with the government of that country while a British army remains in Ireland. Such is the declaration which we call on the people of Ireland to support—And we call first on that part of Ireland which was once paralyzed by the want of intelligence, to shew that to that cause only was its inaction to be attributed; on that part of Ireland which was once foremost, by its fortitude in suffering; on that part of Ireland which once offered to take the salvation of the country on itself; on that part of Ireland where the flame of liberty first glowed; we call upon the NORTH to stand up and shake off their Slumber and their oppression.

MEN OF LEINSTER, STAND TO YOUR ARMS.

To the courage which you have already displayed, is your country indebted for the confidence which it now feels in its own strength, and for the dismay with which our enemies will be overwhelmed when they shall find this effort to be universal. But men of Leinster, you owe more to your country than the having animated it by your past example; you owe more to your own courage, than the having obtained, by it a protection. If six years ago, when you rose without arms, without plan, without cooperation, with more troops against you alone, than are now in the country at large; you were able to remain for six weeks in open defiance of the government, and within a few miles of the capital what will you not now effect, with that capital, and every other part of Ireland ready to support you? But it is not on this head that we have need to address you. No we now speak to you, and through you, to the rest of Ireland, on a subject, dear to us even as the success of our country,—its honour. You are accused by your enemies of having violated that honour; excesses which they themselves had in their fullest extent provoked, but which they have grossly exaggerated, have been attributed to you. The opportunity of vindicating yourselves by actions, is now for the first time before you; and we call upon you to give the lie to such assertions, by carefully avoiding every appearance of plunder, intoxication, or revenge; recollecting that you lost Ireland before, not from want of courage, but from not having that courage rightly directed by discipline. But we trust that your past sufferings, have taught you experience, and that you will respect the declaration which we now make and which we are determined by every means in our power to enforce.

The nation alone possesses the right of punishing individuals, and whosoever shall put another person to death, except in battle, without a fair trial by his country, is guilty of murder. The intention of the provisional government of Ireland, is to claim from the English government, such Irishmen as have been sold or transported, by it for their attachment to freedom; and for this purpose, it will retain as hostages for their safe return, such adherents of that government as shall fall into its hands. It therefore calls upon the people to respect those hostages, and to recollect that in spilling their blood, they would leave their own countrymen in the hands of their enemies.

The intention of the provisional government, is to resign its functions, as soon as the nation shall have chosen its delegates, but in the mean time, it is determined to enforce the regulations hereunto subjoined;—It in consequence takes the property of the country under its protection, and will punish with the utmost rigour any person who shall violate that property, and thereby injure the present resources and the future prosperity of Ireland.

Whoever refuses to march to whatever part of the country he is ordered, is guilty of disobedience to the government, which alone is competent to decide in what place his services are necessary, and which desires him to recollect, that in whatever part of Ireland he is fighting, he is still fighting for its freedom.

Whoever presumes by acts or otherwise to give countenance to the calumny propagated by our enemies, that this is a religious contest, is guilty of the grievous crime of belying the motives of his country. Religious disqualification is but one of the many grievances of which Ireland has to complain. Our intention is to remove not that only, but every other oppression under which we labour. We fight, that all of us may have our country, and that done—each of us shall have his religion.

We are aware of the apprehensions which you have expressed, that in quitting your own counties, you leave your wives and children, in the hands of your enemies; but on this head have no uneasiness. If there are still men base enough to persecute those, who are unable to resist, shew them by your victories that we have the power to punish, and by your obedience, that we have the power to protect, and we pledge ourselves to you, that these men shall be made to feel, that the safety of every thing they hold dear, depends on the conduct they observe to you. Go forth then with confidence, conquer the foreign enemies of your country, and leave to us the care of preserving its internal tranquillity; recollect that not only the victory, but also the honour of your country, is placed in your hands; give up your private resentments, and shew to the world, that the Irish, are not only a brave, but also a generous and forgiving people.

MEN OF MUNSTER AND CONNAUGHT

You have your instructions, we trust that you will execute them. The example of the rest of your countrymen is now before you; your own strength is unbroken;—five months ago you were eager to act without any other assistance. We now call upon you to shew, what you then declared you only wanted the opportunity of proving, that you possess the same love of liberty and the same courage with which the rest of your countrymen are animated.

We now turn to that portion of our countrymen whose prejudices we had rather overcome by a frank declaration of our intentions, than conquer their persons in the field; and in making this declaration, we do not wish to dwell on events, which, however, they may bring tenfold odium on their authors, must still tend to keep alive in the minds both of the instruments and victims of them, a spirit of animosity which it is our wish to destroy. We will therefore enter into no detail of the atrocities and oppression which Ireland has laboured under during its connexion with England; but we justify our determination to separate from that country on the broad historical statement, that during six hundred years she has been unable to conciliate the affections of the people of Ireland; that during that time, five rebellions were entered into, to shake off the yoke; that she has been obliged to resort to a system of unprecedented torture in her defence; that she has broken every tie of voluntary connexion by taking even the name of independence from Ireland, through the intervention of a parliament notoriously bribed, and not representing the will of the people; that in her vindication of this measure she has herself given the justification of the views of the United Irishmen, by declaring in the words of her ministers, "That Ireland never had, and never could "enjoy under the then circumstances the be-"nefit of British connexion; that it necessarily "must happen when one country is connected "with another, that the interests of the lesser "will be borne down by those of the greater.* "That England had supported and encouraged "the English colonists in their oppression to-"wards the natives of Ireland; that Ireland "had been left in a state of ignorance, rude-"ness and barbarism, worse in its effects, and "more degrading in its nature, than that in "which it was found six centuries before."† Now to what cause are these things to be attributed? Did the curse of the almighty keep alive a spirit of obstinacy in the minds of the Irish people for six hundred years? Did the doctrines of the French revolution produce five rebellions? Could the misrepresentations of ambitious and designing men drive from the mind of a whole people, the recollection of defeat, and raise the infant from the cradle, with the same feelings with which his father sunk into the grave? Will this gross avowal which our enemies have made of their own views, remove none of the calumny that has been thrown upon ours? Will none of the credit has been lavished on them, be transferred to the solemn declaration which we now make in the face of god and our country. We war not against property—We war against no religious sect—We war not against past opinions or prejudices—We war against English dominion. We will not however deny, that there are some men, who, not because they have supported the government of our oppressors, but because they have violated the common laws of morality, which exist alike under all or under no government; have put it beyond our power to give to them the protection of a government. We will not hazard the influence we may have with the people, and the power it may give us of preventing the excesses of revolution, by undertaking to place in tranquillity the man who has been guilty of torture, free quarters, rape and murder, by the side of the sufferer or their relations; but in the frankness with which we warn these men of their danger, let those who do not feel that they have passed this boundary of mediation, count on their safety.

We had hoped for the sake of our enemies to have taken them by surprize, and to have committed the cause of our country before they could have time to commit themselves against it; but though we have not altogether been able to succeed, we are yet rejoiced to find that they have not come forward with promptitude on the side of those who have deceived them, and we now call on them before it is yet too late, not to commit themselves further against a people they are unable to resist, and in support of a government, which, by their own declaration has forfeited its claim to their allegiance.

To that government in whose hands, though not the issue, at least the features with which the present contest is to be marked, are placed, we now turn. How is it to be decided? is open and honourable force alone to be resorted to, or is it your intention to employ those laws which custom has placed in your hands, and to force us to employ the law of retaliation in our defence?

Of the inefficacy of a system of terror, in preventing the people of Ireland from coming forward to assert their freedom, you have already had experience. Of the effect which such a system will have on our minds in case of success, we have already forewarned you—We now address to you another consideration—If in the question which is now to receive a solemn and we trust final decision, if we have been deceived reflection would point out that conduct should be resorted to, which was the best calculated to produce conviction on our minds. What would that conduct be? It would be to shew to us that the difference of strength between the two countries is such, as to render it unnecessary for you to bring out all your force; to shew to us that you have something in reserve wherewith to crush hereafter, not only a greater exertion on the part of the people, but a greater exertion, rendered still greater by foreign assistance: It would be to shew to us that what we have vainly supposed to be a prosperity growing beyond your grasp, is only a partial exuberance requiring but the pressure of your hand to reduce it into form. But for your own sake do not resort to a system, which while it increased the acrimony of our minds would leave us under the melancholy delusion that we had been forced to yield, not to the sound and temperate exertions of superior strength, but to the frantick struggles of weakness, concealing itself under desperation. Consider also that the distinction of rebel and enemy is of a very fluctuating nature; that during the course of your own experience you have already been obliged to lay it aside; that should you be forced to abandon it towards Ireland you cannot hope to do so as tranquilly as you have done towards America, for in the exasperated state to which you have raised the minds of the Irish people; a people whom you profess to have left in a state of barbarism and ignorance, with what confidence can you say to that people "while "the advantage of cruelty lay upon our side, "we slaughtered you without mercy, but the "measure of our own blood is beginning to "preponderate, it is no longer our interest that "this bloody system should continue, shew us "then, that forbearance which we never taught "you by precept or example, lay aside your "resentments, give quarter to us, and let us "mutually forget, that we never gave quarter "to you." Cease then we entreat you uselessly to violate humanity by resorting to a system inefficacious as an instrument of terror, inefficacious as a mode of defence, inefficacious as a mode of conviction, ruinous to the future relations of the two countries in case of our success, and destructive of those instruments of defence which you will then find it doubly necessary to have preserved unimpaired. But if your determination be otherwise, hear ours. We will not imitate you in cruelty; we will put no man to death in cold blood, the prisoners which first fall into our hands shall be treated with the respect due to the unfortunate; but if the life of a single Irish soldier is taken after the battle is over, the orders thence forth to be issued to the Irish army are neither to give or take quarter. Countrymen if a cruel necessity forces us to retaliate, we will bury our resentments in the field of battle, if we are to fall, we will fall where we fight for our country—Fully impressed with this determination, of the necessity of adhering to which past experience has but too fatally convinced us; fully impressed with the justice of our cause which we now put to issue. We make our last and solemn appeal to the sword and to Heaven; and as the cause of Ireland deserves to prosper, may God give it Victory.

Conformably to the above proclamation, the Provisional Government of Ireland, decree that as follows.

1. From the date and promulgation hereof, tithes are for ever abolished, and church lands are the property of the nation.
2. From the same date, all transfers of landed property are prohibited, each person, holding what he now possesses, on paying his rent until the national government is established, the national will declared, and the courts of justice organized.
3. From the same date, all transfer of Bonds, debentures, and all public securities, are in like manner and form forbidden, and declared void, for the same time, and for the same reasons.
4. The Irish generals commanding districts, shall seize such of the partizans of England as may serve for hostages, and shall apprize the English commander opposed to them, that a strict retaliation shall take place if any outrages contrary to the laws of war shall be committed by the troops under his command, or by the partizans of England in the district which he occupies.
5. That the Irish generals are to treat (except where retaliation makes it necessary) the English troops who may fall into their hands, or such Irish as serve in the regular forces of England, and who shall have acted conformably to the laws of war, as prisoners of war; but all Irish militia, yeomen, or volunteer corps, or bodies of Irish, or individuals, who fourteen days from the promulgation and date hereof, shall be found in arms, shall be considered as rebels, committed for trial, and their properties confiscated.
6. The generals are to assemble court-martials, who are to be sworn to administer justice; who are not to condemn without sufficient evidence, and before whom all military offenders are to be sent instantly for trial.
7. No man is to suffer death by their sentence, except for mutiny; the sentences of such others as are judged worthy of death, shall not be put in execution until the provisional government declares its will, nor are court-martials on any pretext to sentence, nor is any officer to suffer the punishment of flogging, or any species of torture, to be inflicted.
8. The generals are to enfore the strictest discipline, and to send offenders immediately before court-martials, and are enjoined to chace away from the Irish armies all such as shall disgrace themselves by being drunk in presence of the enemy.
9. The generals are to apprize their respective armies, that all military stores, arms, or ammunition, belonging to the English government, be the property of the captors and the value is to be divided equally without respect of rank between them, except that the widows, orphans, parents, or other heirs of such as gloriously fall in the attack, shall be entitled to a double share.
10. As the English nation has made war on Ireland, all English property in ships or otherwise, is subject to the same rule, and all transfer of them is forbidden and declared void, in like manner as is expressed in No. 2 and 3.
11. The generals of the different districts are hereby empowered to confer rank up to colonels inclusive, on such as they conceive to merit it from the nation, but are not to make more colonels than one for fifteen hundred men, nor more Lieutenant-Colonels than one for every thousand men,
12. The generals shall seize on all sums of public money in the custom-houses in their districts, or in the hands of the different collectors, county treasurers, or other revenue officers, whom they shall render responsible for the sums in their hands. The generals shall pass receipts for the amount, and account to the provisional government for the expenditure.
13. When the people elect their officers up to the colonels, the general is bound to confirm it—no officer can be broke but by sentence of a court-martial.
14. The generals shall correspond with the provisional government, to whom they shall give details of all their operations, they are to correspond with the neighbouring generals to whom they are to transmit all necessary intelligence, and to co-operate with them,
15. The generals commanding in each county shall as soon as it is cleared of the enemy, assemble the county committee, who shall be elected conformably to the constitution of United Irishmen, all the requisitions necessary for the army shall be made in writing by the generals to the committee, who are hereby empowered and enjoined to pass their receipts for each article to the owners, to the end that they may receive their full value from the nation.
16. The county committee is charged with the civil direction of the county, the care of the national property, and the preservation of order and justice in the county; for which purpose the county committees are to appoint a high-sheriff, and one or more sub-sheriffs to execute their orders, a sufficient number of justices of the peace for the county, a high and a sufficient number of petty constables in each barony, who are respectively charged with the duties now performed by these magistrates.
17. The county of Cork on account of its extent, is to be divided conformably to the boundaries for raising the militia into the counties of north and south Cork, for each of which a county constable, high-sheriff and all magistrates above directed are to be appointed.
18. The county committee are hereby empowered and enjoined to issue warrants to apprehend such persons as it shall appear, on sufficient evidence perpetrated murder, torture, or other breaches of the acknowledged laws of war and morality on the people, to the end that they may be tried for those offences, so soon as the competent courts of justice are established by the nation.
19. The county committee shall cause the sheriff or his officers to seize on all the personal and real property of such persons, to put seals on their effects, to appoint proper persons to preserve all such property until the national courts of justice shall have decided on the fate of the proprietors.
20. The county committee shall act in like manner, with all state and church lands, parochial estates, and all public lands and edifices.
21. The county committee shall in the interim receive all the rents and debts of such persons and estates, and shall give receipts for the same, shall transmit to the provisional government an exact account of their value, extent and amount, and receive the directions of the provisional government thereon.
22. They shall appoint some proper house in the counties where the sheriff is permanently to reside, and where the county committee shall assemble, they shall cause all the records and papers of the county to be there transferred, arranged, and kept, and the orders of government are there to be transmitted and received.
23. The county committee is hereby empowered to pay out of these effects, or by assessment, reasonable salaries for themselves, the sheriff justices and other magistrates whom they shall appoint.
24. They shall keep a written journal of all their proceedings signed each day by the members of the committee, or a sufficient number of them for the inspection of government.
25. The county committee shall correspond with government on all the subjects with which they are charged, and transmit to the general of the district such information as they may conceive useful to the public.
26. The county committee shall take care that the state prisoners, however great their offences, shall be treated with humanity, and allow them a sufficient support to the end that all the world may know, that the Irish nation is not actuated by the spirit of revenge, but of justice.
27. The provisional government wishing to commit as soon as possible the sovereign authority to the people, direct that each county and city shall elect agreeably to the constitution of United Irishmen, representatives to meet in Dublin, to whom the moment they assemble the provisional government will resign its functions; and without presuming to dictate to the people, they beg to suggest, that for the important purpose to which these electors are called, integrity of character should be the first object.
28. The number of representatives being arbitrary, the provisional government have adopted that of the late house of commons, three hundred, and according to the best return of the population of the cities and counties the following numbers are to be returned from each:—Antrim 13—Armagh 9—Belfast town 1—Carlow 3—Cavan 7—Clare 8 Cork county, north 14—Cork co. south 14—Cork city 6—Donegal 10—Down 16—Drogheda 1—Dublin county 4—Dublin city 14—Fermanagh 5—Galway 10—Kerry 9—Kildare 4—Kilkenny 7—King's county 6—Leitrim 5—Limerick county 10—Limerick city 3—Londonderry 9—Longford 4—Louth 4—Mayo 12—Meath 9—Monaghan 9—Queen's county 6—Roscommon 8—Sligo 6—Tipperary 13—Tyrone 14—Waterford county 6—Waterford city 2—Westmeath 5—Wexford 9—Wicklow 5—
29. In the cities the same sort of regulations as in the counties shall be adopted; the city committee shall appoint one or more sheriffs as they think proper, and shall take possession of all the public and corporation properties in their jurisdiction in like manner as is directed for counties.
30. The provisional government strictly exhort and enjoin all magistrates, officers, civil and military, and the whole of the nation, to cause the laws of Morality to be enforced and respected, and to execute as far as in them lies justice with mercy, by whcih alone liberty can be established, and the blessings of divine providence secured.

* Lord Castlereagh's speech.

† Considerations on the state of affairs in Ireland, by lord Auckland

Proclamation of the Provisional Government (NAI, Rebellion Papers, 620/11/134).

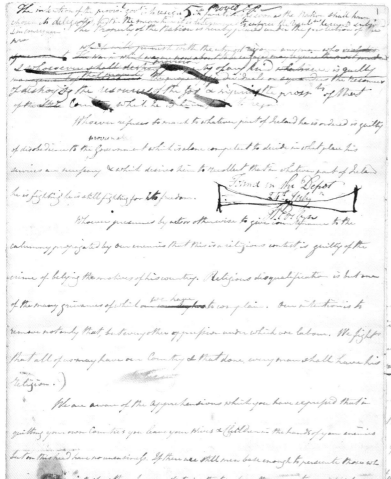

Draft Proclamation of the Provisional Government (NAI, Rebellion Papers, 620/12/155/3).

Having decided to make an armed showing in Thomas Street, Emmet emerged from the main depot at around 9.30pm and read extracts from a proclamation setting down the political agenda and motivation of the United Irishmen. Manuscript drafts may have been circulated earlier by Russell and Hope in Ulster, but those issued in the capital were printed in 62 Abbey Street by John Stockdale on the afternoon of the revolt. The proclamation reflected the input of Addis Emmet, MacNeven, Russell and Dowdall and revealed how American and French democratic principles would be applied in Ireland. Its provisions included highly progressive statements of human rights, the electorate and constituencies.

William Gue...

CITIZENS OF DUBLIN.

A BAND of PATRIOTS, mindful of their OATH and faithful to their engagement as UNITED IRISHMEN, have determined to give freedom to their country, and a period to the long career of ENGLISH oppression.

In this endeavour they are now succesfully engaged; and their efforts are seconded by complete and universal co-operation from the country, every part of which, from the extremity of the *North*, to that of the *South*, pours forth its warriors in support of our hallowed cause. Citizens of Dublin, we require your aid; necessary secrecy has prevented to many of you, notice of our plan, but the erection of our NATIONAL STANDARD, the secret, though long *degraded Green*, will be found sufficient call to arms, and rally round it every man in whose breast exists a spark of *Patriotism*; or sense of duty; avail of your local advantages; in a city each Street become a defile; and each House a Battery; impede the march of your oppressors, charge them with the Arms of the brave, the Pike, and from your Windows and Roofs, hurl stones, Bricks, Bottles, and all other convenient implements on the heads of the satalites of your Tyrant, the mercenary, the sanguinary Soldiery of ENGLAND.

ORANGEMEN add not to the catalogue of your follies and crimes; already have you been duped to the ruin of your Country, in the Legislative Union with its Tyrant; attempt not an opposition which will carry with it, your inevitable destruction, return from the paths of delusion, return to the arms of your Countrymen, who will receive and hail your repentance.

COUNTRYMEN of all descriptions, let us act with Union and concert; all sects, Catholic, Protestant, Presbyterian are equally and indiscriminately embraced in the benevolence of our object; repress, prevent, and discourage excesses, pillage and intoxication; let each man do his duty, and remember that during public agitation inaction becomes a crime; be no other competition known than that of doing good; remember against whom you fight, your oppressors for six hundred years; *remember their massacres, their tortures, remember* your *murdered friends*, your *burned houses*, your *violated females*; keep in mind your COUNTRY, to whom we are now giving her high rank among Nations, and in the honest terror of feeling, let us all exclaim that as in the hour of her *trial* we serve this COUNTRY, so may GOD serve us in that which will be last of all!

'**Citizens of Dublin**' (NAI, Rebellion Papers, 620/12/155/5).

The Corn Market House, Thomas Street, Dublin by Charles Brooking, engraved by John Bowles (NGI, 10,015 (18)).

Overleaf
July 23, 1803. Robert Emmet heads his men by J.D. Reigh (*Shamrock*, 5 July 1890).

Thomas Street Market House was one of the main focal points of the Rising of 1803, a factor that resulted in its subsequent fortification. Emmet had decided to countermand the orders to rise before he approached the building. The single rocket fired at around 9.15pm prompted those watching in the suburbs and around the city to disperse immediately. Similarly, heavily armed groups of veterans awaiting final orders in Wood Quay, Ship Street and Costigan's Distillery on Thomas Street were not contacted by Emmet before the approach to the Castle. This indicates that Emmet's officers wished to draw low-ranking rebels away from Thomas Street, where two dragoons had been killed, and toward the Dublin Mountains, where they could hold out until the French arrived.

The address to the citizens of Dublin, dictated to Michael Meighan by Philip Long, was in the tradition of the inflammatory document drafted by John Sheares in May 1798. Its purpose was to exhort the rank-and-file United Irishmen instructed to assemble in Thomas Street at 6.00pm to undertake the dangerous tasks expected of them after 9.00pm.

91

Denis Lambert Redmond **by James Petrie** (NLI, EP REDM-DE (1) 11).

Wexford, Wicklow and Dublin city rebels gathered in the Coal Quay (Wood Quay) home of Denis Lambert Redmond on the evening of 23 July 1803. Miles Byrne and William Darcy, leaders of the well-equipped Rebellion veterans in Redmond's house, were not called upon by Emmet to storm the Castle.

Great Court Yard, Dublin Castle by James **Malton** (NLI, PD 3181 TX 37).

92

The gates of Dublin Castle, a lightly defended complex in 1803, were left open during the Rising. Marsden's failure to summon the Privy Council, however, lessened the value of seizing the Castle, a circumstance that may have had bearing on Emmet's deliberations.

Entrance to Upper Castle Yard (NLI, 1963 (TX) 25(A)).

Arthur Wolfe, Viscount Killwarden [sic] (NLI, EP KILW-AR (3) 11).

John Byrne's map of Newlands, Co. Kildare, 1802 (NLI, MS 12 G 16 (47)).

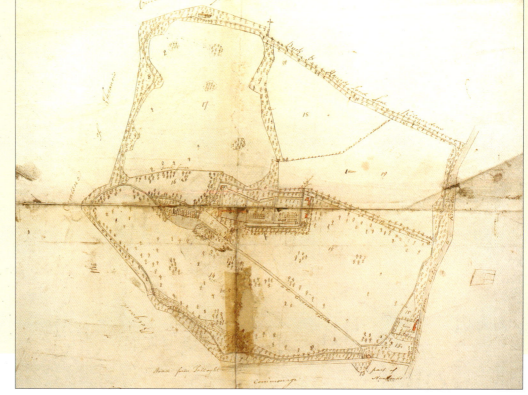

The murder of Lord Kilwarden by George Cruikshank (NLI, HP (1798) 14 (A)).

95

Chief Justice Kilwarden spurned offers of refuge in Guinness's compound at James's Gate just before being piked to death near the Vicar Street corner of Thomas Street. The judge had failed to comply with the demands of rebels who were eager to prevent carriages overtaking them on the way to the Castle. Revd Richard Wolfe, Kilwarden's nephew, was also fatally piked, but his daughter Elizabeth was unharmed. Colonel John Finlay, a near neighbour, had warned of trouble in the city, and the Wolfes unwisely sought refuge in the Castle. Kilwarden's death convinced Emmet that the Rising could not succeed.

County of Dublin }
to wit }

The Information of Rich.ᵈ Wornall, of Patrick Street, Victualler.

Who, being duly sworn & examined saith, that about twilight on the evening of Saturday, the 23.ᵈ July last, he saw a Man march down Plunket Street, into Patrick Street at the head of 14 or 15 men; that when he entered Patrick he halted, and x addressed the people in the Street saying "Turn out my boys, now is your time for Liberty — Liberty my boys — now turn out!". That said person then fired a pistol into the air, and immediately marched towards Kivin Street, at the head of his party, which he commanded. That said person was dressed in a white Jacket, faced with green, and laced with gold, with a pair of large Gold Epaulets, and wore a very large Cocked hat with a long green feather. to the best of Inf.ᵗˢ belief. That in a few minutes after said party marched off, another party of about 300 Men marched also down Plunket Street, and in their way broke every lamp in Informant view; that on their entering Patrick Street they set up a most savage Yell, and demanded to know which way the former party went; and, on being informed by some persons in the Street, they marched in the same direction. That the whole of said parties were armed with long white poles, which Inf.ᵗ is now convinced were pikes. That the man who command said first party appeared to Inf.ᵗ to be from 30 to 40 years old, and was from about five feet seven or five feet eight inches in height, and his dress was most superb.

Sworn before me
30.ᵈ Aug.ᵗ 1803

Richard Wornall

Information of Richard Wornall
(NAI, Rebellion Papers, 620/11/129/14).

Richard Wornall, a Patrick Street shopkeeper, observed the movements of various rebel groups through the south city after Emmet's staff had headed out the Harold's Cross Road toward Rathfarnham.

APPENDIX *to the* Report *from* Commiffioners *on*

Appendix,
No. 10,
continued.

Complaints.

all your Memorialift's ftock in trade and houfehold furniture were actually fold by auction, by the Sheriffs of the County of the City of Dublin, to the complete ruin and deftruction of your Memorialift, at a period when your Memorialift was lying incarcerated in clofe and rigorous confinement, without having an opportunity of communicating with fuch perfons as might alleviate his heavy diftreffes, and relieve him from his then extreme wants and miferies.

That about the hour of ten of the clock on the night of the twenty-third day of July, one thoufand eight hundred and three, as your Memorialift was fitting at home at John-ftreet aforefaid, a private of the twenty-firft or Royal Scotch Fufileers, whofe name was Robert Burgefs, being unarmed, together with two of his regiment, which two were killed on faid laft-mentioned night, happened to come running down John-ftreet aforefaid, and a Clerk of your Memorialift being infide the door of faid concerns, faid Robert Burgefs cried out for mercy, whereupon your Memorialift's faid Clerk immediately opened the door and let him in, and brought him to your Memorialift in the houfe; upon which your Memorialift made him fit down, and told him he fhould be taken care of, and that he need not be under any apprehenfion whatever, and accordingly gave him fome refrefhment and a bed that night.

That faid Robert Burgefs, feeling grateful for your Memorialift having fo kindly protected him on the night of the infurrection aforefaid, called repeatedly to return your Memorialift thanks; and having at one time called after your Memorialift had been fo arrefted as aforefaid, and being informed that your Memorialift was confined in the Provoft, he immediately declared he would do any thing in his power to ferve your Memorialift, fo as to extricate him from his then confinement, and accordingly faid Burgefs informed his Officers thereof, and confulted them thereupon, and by and with the advice and directions, as your Memorialift verily believes, went before Humphrey Minchin, efq. formerly high Sheriff of the City of Dublin, and Jofeph Minchin, efq. his fon drew faid Burgefs's affidavit, ftating the fervices your Memorialift had rendered him, and that your Memorialift was the means of faving his life, together with other circumftances which your Memorialift cannot at prefent recollect; which faid affidavit faid Burgefs fwore before faid Humphrey Minchin, and was minutely interrogated both by faid Minchin and his fon relative to your Memorialift, which proved highly fatisfactory to them; all of which faid Humphrey Minchin and his faid fon can verify if required.

Extract from *Parliamentary Papers*, 1809, p. 118.

The first contest on Thomas Street between the rebels and Second Lieutenant Felix Brady's detachment of the 21st Regiment ended with the soldiers retreating into James's Street Barracks. When rebel forces under Owen Kirwan, Patrick McCabe, Thomas Keogh and others converged on the Coombe Barracks, a series of skirmishes with the Regiment's light company commenced. Captain Stuart Hume Douglas, backed by elements of the Liberty Rangers, inflicted far more casualties than he sustained but ultimately withdrew to barracks. The death of soldiers and the panic that gripped city loyalists were played down in official accounts.

The Rt. Hon. Lord Henry Fitzgerald (NLI, EP FITZ-HE (1) 1).

Significant rebel activity in Kildare led to the capture of Celbridge and Maynooth. This mirrored the cutting-off of Dublin's radial roads at Sandymount, Ballsbridge, Phibsborough and Rathfarnham but received much greater attention owing to suspicions that the Fitzgeralds of Carton and the Catholic clergy in Maynooth seminary were complicit. The liberal Edgeworth family was perturbed by the conduct of the yeomen during searches in Kildare.

98

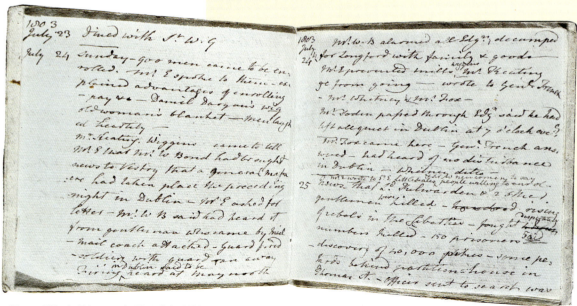

Diary of Maria Edgeworth, 23–5 July 1803 (NLI, MS 18,752).

'Heroines of Irish history. V: The torture of Anne Devlin' (*Irish Fireside*, 5 August 1885).

99

Anne Devlin in silhouette (NMI).

Devlin was displeased when Emmet's group returned to Rathfarnham to bury an arms cache and make contact with Dwyer's Wicklowmen. She and her sister were severely maltreated by the local yeomanry on 26 July 1803 but did not divulge the whereabouts of the leading insurgents hiding in the Ballynameece/Bohernabreena area.

Chapter 5

Trials and executions

The scale and duration of the crackdown that followed the Rising of 1803 testified to the seriousness with which it was regarded in Dublin and London. Although confined to much narrower bounds than its potential, the fact that several hundred United Irishmen had assembled in a capital city during wartime and without opposition from a garrison of 4000 regulars suggested that something had gone terribly wrong in the Castle and army headquarters. The Act of Union ensured that the repercussions of this lapse were investigated in Westminster, where Castlereagh and other leading politicians went to great pains to prevent a full and frank examination of the causes of the Rising in the Houses of Parliament. In the short term, the Commons and the Lords rushed through emergency legislation on 28 July permitting the imposition of martial law and suspension of *habeas corpus* in Ireland. This led to the most concerted anti-insurgent drive since 1797–8.

Soldiers, watchmen and yeomen were directed to enter houses in search of suspected revolutionaries and their hidden arms caches. Committal rates were such that the Provost, Kilmainham, Newgate and other holding centres were quickly overwhelmed and auxiliary prison tenders had to be moored in Dublin Bay. Men whose names had appeared in the reports of magistrates and secret agents after 1798, together with those deemed likely to have played a part in the events of 23 July 1803, were taken from their homes to face an uncertain fate. Mass arrests in Kildare, Wicklow and County Dublin filled regional jails, while the magistrates in the provinces were encouraged to use the *carte blanche* of martial law to smash the United Irish infrastructure. In Cork and Limerick, disturbed counties where no combat had occurred in 1803, the most prominent Republicans to have escaped the fallout of 1798 were the primary targets. This was also the case in Belfast, Downpatrick, Ballymena and other Northern towns that had been approached by armed rebel columns that did not engage the military. Newry magistrates also petitioned for a prison tender in Carlingford Bay. All counties affected by the 1798 Rebellion witnessed mass arrests and the aggressive patrolling of state agents who were immune from prosecution.

Robert Emmet spurned offers of hiding-places in the Wicklow Mountains and Kildare and returned to his Harold's Cross lodgings to coordinate the United Irish response to the crisis. Miles Byrne was sent to France to urge an invasion at the earliest possible moment, and, while arrests decimated the organisation in the city and beyond, the leadership was undoubtedly reassured that its security-consciousness temporarily shielded the upper tier of commanders. The arrest of Emmet in Harold's Cross on 25 August, however, followed by that of Russell in 28 Parliament Street, Dublin, on 9 September, delivered the *coup de grâce* to the conspiracy. The remaining leaders went to ground to await deliverance by the French, who, unbeknownst to them, lacked the resources to mount the invasion planned for early autumn. Allen and Dowdall escaped to France, but Long, Redmond, Rourke and several other city-based figures were seized within weeks. Although Emmet, Russell, Redmond and Rourke were the only senior men to suffer death, dozens of their followers were executed in September/October 1803 by the Special Commissions of Dublin and Downpatrick.

The death toll would have been much higher had the Castle not been embarrassed by its failure to pre-empt the Rising and under pressure from Westminster to present a confident position to the attentive French. The authorities were consequently satisfied with the conviction of secondary leaders and their rank-and-file followers. This enabled the Castle to project the false impression, superficially bolstered by the relatively modest parameters of the July uprising, that the United Irishmen had failed to harness popular support and were in terminal decline. Emmet was disposed to accept a greater degree of responsibility and blame than appropriate by his desire to protect subordinates, as well as his secret fiancée, Sarah Curran, whom he had inadvertently implicated in correspondence. Emmet was thus prepared to enter into an understanding with William Wickham and offered no real defence when brought to trial for high treason in Green Street Courthouse on 19 September 1803. His famous 'speech from the dock', nonetheless, broadcast the existence of a reformed United Irish Directory and explained the nature of their negotiations with the French. This displeased Judge John Toler (Lord Norbury), who interrupted the vindication and confiscated its text. Crucially, Emmet challenged his contemporaries to continue the struggle to bring an independent Irish Republic into being with foreign military assistance. Such sentiments had not been heard since 1798 and confirmed to all that the United Irish project retained its relevance after Union with Britain.

Also significant, if more disingenuous, was an account of the conspiracy written by Emmet in Kilmainham on the eve of execution. The ostensible recipient was the exiled Thomas Addis Emmet, but the real purpose of the document was to attune the establishment to the revolutionary potential of the United Irishmen. This implicit threat, mirroring the more provocative passages of his curtailed trial speech, warned the authorities to temper the severity of their counter-insurgency programme or face the consequences. A similar warning was verbally conveyed by Emmet to Leonard MacNally, Jnr, when awaiting execution. It is evident that Emmet succeeded in unnerving the government, given that the official version of the 'speech from the dock' was edited and censored and the even more unsettling 'account' was totally suppressed. On 20 September Emmet was taken under heavy guard to a Thomas Street scaffold. The circuitous route brought him past the Royal Barracks on the north bank of the Liffey and back into the south city via Bridgefoot Street. He was hanged and beheaded in front of a huge crowd on a specially constructed platform erected in front of St Catherine's Church. After a period on display in Kilmainham prison, his decollated remains were buried in Hospital Fields (Bully's Acre) by the Roscommon Militia. The body was removed within days to St Michan's, Church Street, and, by the time of its third interment in March 1805, Emmet had gained the celebrity and notoriety that distinguished him as the most discussed Irishman of the nineteenth century.

Rewards offered by the Privy Council (*Dublin Gazette*, 23–6 July 1803).

The Privy Council convened emergency sessions in Dublin Castle to offer substantial rewards for apprehending the killers of soldiers, yeomen, loyalists and Lord Kilwarden.

of the services of 1803, 4,500,000l. of which remained to be paid off. If the committee acceded to the present motion, there would also be an opportunity for the issue of new exchequer bills, for which there was now a considerable demand. So much would consequently be taken from the supply of the year; but the whole of what he now moved for would be necessary for the public service, till the advanced period of the session, when the whole of the supply was voted. If particular information was called for on any of these points, he should be ready to give every explanation in his power. He concluded by moving, " that the sum of five millions be raised by loan on exchequer bills, for the service of the year 1804." This motion being agreed to, the house resumed, and the report was ordered to be received to-morrow.

[SUSPENSION OF HABEAS CORPUS ACT IN IRELAND.]—Mr. *Secretary Yorke.* I rise, Sir, in consequence of a notice which I gave a few days ago, for leave to bring in two bills to continue two acts; the one for suspending the Habeas Corpus Act, and the other for the re-enactment of Martial Law in Ireland. The house may be assured, that it is with the sincerest regret for the circumstances which render this measure necessary, that I now come forward to perform this painful duty. I am sorry to be obliged to propose any measure that may trench upon the liberties of the subject, or any of those blessings which this country justly values at so high a rate. But, Sir, it is the misfortune of the times in which we are destined to live, that we are not permitted to enjoy our lives, our liberties, or our possessions, without being daily called upon to sacrifice some part of our privileges in order to preserve the remainder, to sacrifice the best blood of the country in support of the contest in which we are engaged, and to abridge our liberties in order to preserve the existence of liberty itself. But this is no more than our ancestors often thought proper to do. There exists, however, this lamentable difference, that the periods during which it was necessary to resort to measures of this sort, were extremely short with them; but we can never rest in complete security, nor think either our privileges or our lives in safety, while France, after spreading devastation and death over her tributaries on the continent, looks with malignant envy on this happy spot, and longs to extend her fiend-like fangs to crush us also, and level us

VOL. IV.

with the lowest of her slaves. It will be needless for me to state more particularly than I have done, the object of these bills. It will be recollected that they passed towards the conclusion of last session, in consequence of a message from his Majesty, stating the insurrection that had broken out in the city of Dublin, and the atrocious circumstances with which it was attended. The house very properly passed those acts without any hesitation; when passed, they gave confidence to the loyal inhabitants of Ireland, and enabled them to suppress the rebellion with celerity. The particular circumstances which gave rise to and accompanied that most unhappy transaction, has now been developed by the trials of several of the leaders and their adherents, before the ordinary courts of judicature, and according to the ordinary forms of law. The proceedings on these occasions have been published, and to them I refer the house for information whereon to found their judgment, as to the nature and extent of the conspiracy, as well as to the expediency of the present motion. Exclusive of the information contained in these trials, his Majesty's government are in possession of other facts, which the house must feel it would be highly improper to attempt to detail at the present moment. I may, however, be permitted to state, that notwithstanding the declaration of one of them (Emmett), I have every reason to believe, that the leaders of that insurrection were connected with persons residing in France, and those persons, traitors, immediately connected with the French government, if the conspirators were not immediately connected with it themselves. It is also clear, that some of the traitors who were in France, came over to Ireland for the purpose of exciting rebellion, and that they calculated upon the renewal of hostilities between this country and France, and chose that moment for exciting rebellion, as the most favourable crisis for putting in execution their nefarious designs. It is, indeed, clear, from all that has come to the knowledge of government, that the great object of the French government was to foster and increase treason and rebellion in Ireland, with a hope of distracting and dividing the British empire, and finally leading to the subversion of the country: but the perfidy of the enemy was defeated, and his hope was vain. With respect to the events of the 23d of July, the details are before the public, and it is not necessary to enlarge upon them. The

* P p

horrid tale is known; and, perhaps, in all the history of violence, madness, and folly which the world ever presented; there never existed treason more foul, an insurrection more unprovoked, leaders more contemptible, assassination more atrocious, or crimes more horrible.—What followed is extremely well known: most of the leaders have been brought to justice before the ordinary tribunals, which these miscreants wished to put an end to, and exterminate; as evidently appears by their horrible assassination of one of the brightest ornaments of those tribunals. I hope my right hon. friend (the Chancellor of the Exchequer) will shortly have it in command from his Majesty, to lay the situation of the family of the much respected, and much lamented nobleman to whom I have alluded (Kilwarden), before the house.—Sir, it becomes my duty to propose the continuance of the acts in question, and I hope that, as far as concerns the manner in which these acts have been made use of, there will be no objection. All the criminals have, notwithstanding the powers vested in the Irish government, been tried in the ordinary form, except in one solitary instance, where a person who endeavoured to seduce a soldier from his allegiance, was justly and properly tried by martial law. Of the necessity for these measures no man can entertain a doubt, who has taken any trouble to make himself acquainted with the state of Ireland, or who is at all aware of the views of the French government, with whom it has been a long favoured plan to attack the empire on the side of Ireland. The enemy is aware that it is only by dividing and diverting the strength of this country, that she can insure success; for united, the British empire single handed, is more than a match for all France. Provided government be on their guard, there is little reason to fear either foreign or domestic enemies. As to the latter, indeed, I am persuaded there are few, very few now to be found in this country. I regret that there are more in Ireland, although their numbers are greatly diminished. But let their numbers be great or small, they must be met with firmness and resolution. They must be made sensible that this house will never compromise with traitors, nor suffer them to clothe themselves with the whole armour of the law, whilst they are secretly attacking the government, and the senate, and all loyal subjects, with the concealed weapons of assassination.—I therefore move, Sir, " that

leave be given to bring in a bill to continue, for a time to be limited, the suspension of the Habeas Corpus act in Ireland."

The Hon. *C. Hely Hutchinson.*—With most of the sentiments expressed by the right hon. gent. who has just sat down, I rise to declare my perfect concurrence; and I am happy to feel justified in assuring the house, that the conduct of the government of Ireland since the insurrection, meets with my entire approbation. Their firmness and humanity; their activity and attention, entitle them to the utmost praise. They have in a great measure pursued that line of policy, which the wise and just would always recommend to be observed towards Ireland. Their temper and lenity have tended to cultivate the good opinion of the people; which was precisely the course, which, at the close of the last session of parliament, I had entreated should be adopted; an exhortation by me, which seemed to have been much misconceived, and for offering which, I became the subject of severe and unmerited censure, from particular quarters: several paragraphs (I should be ashamed to suppose from authority) were inserted in some of the Dublin papers, and also in those of this city, tending to decry the individual who had attempted to call the attention of parliament to the affairs of Ireland. I was quite unconscious, on that occasion, of having given any provocation to the friends of the noble earl, at the head of the government of that country. Such was not my object; as it was, and is, matter of indifference to me, by whom the offices of state are filled, provided government be well administered: in the mode of that administration I am, so far as relates to Ireland, particularly interested. Connected to her by all the sacred ties which can bind an individual to his country, strengthened by a respect for the talents, a regard for the virtues, and a warm sympathy in the wishes of its inhabitants: eager as I feel for their welfare, rejoicing in their prosperity, and participating in their afflictions, I cannot but sincerely lament the necessity which ministers feel themselves under, for again resorting to parliament, for the measures now proposed. But, that under the present circumstances of that unhappy country, it is advisable thus to strengthen the hands of the executive, I cannot entertain a doubt: and I feel the less reluctance in again entrusting the Irish government with these extraordinary powers, when I reflect upon the moderation and lenity with which they have li-

'Suspension of Habeas Corpus Act in Ireland' (*Cobbett's Parliamentary Debates*, 1803–4 (London, 1804), vol. 1, pp 1585–7).

The hurried adoption of coercion laws in London on 28 July 1803 necessitated ignoring the standing orders of the Houses of Parliament. Coercion was continued after periodic renewal until early 1806.

John Philpot Curran by Henry Brocas, Snr (NLI, BR 2115 TX 79).

Peter Burrowes
(courtesy of Peter Burrowes and The Robert Emmet Association).

Burrowes and Curran, senior barristers sympathetic to the United Irishmen in the 1790s, defended United Irish prisoners in 1803 while deploring the killing of Kilwarden. Curran refused to represent Emmet, however, owing to his additional disapproval of the revolutionary's relationship with his daughter. The Priory, Rathfarnham, was raided by Major Sirr on 9 September 1803.

Charles Kendal Bushe (NLI, Barrington).

Leonard MacNally, engraved by Patrick Maguire (NLI, EP MCNA-LE 1).

Bushe, an Emmet family friend, appeared in court on behalf of imprisoned Republicans in 1803. MacNally, also acquainted with leading United Irishmen, subordinated the interests of his clients to those of the government, which he secretly assisted.

A RETURN of PERSONS who have been detained in the Gaol at KILMAINHAM since the 23d day of July 1803, under the Authority of the Acts passed in the last and preceding Sessions of Parliament, empowering the Lord Lieutenant or other Chief Governor or Governors of Ireland to apprehend and detain such Persons as he or they shall suspect of conspiring against His Majesty's Person and Government.

NAMES of PRISONERS.	CHARGES against them, as expressed in the Warrant.	Whether the Informations were on Oath, as stated in the Warrant.	Length of TIME in Custody.		HOW DISPOSED OF.	FUNDS by which Maintained during Confinement.
N°			From	To		
1. Carter Connelly	High Treason	Not stated	28th July 1803	28th Jan. 1804	Discharged by order of Gov^t	Paid by the Crown Solicitor.
2. Gerald Hope	Ditto	Ditto	28th Ditto	27th Sept. 1803	Ditto.	Ditto
3. John Palmer	D°	D°	D°	Still in Confinement	- - - -	D°
4. John Stockdale	D°	D°	29th Ditto	23d Jan. 1804	Discharged by order of Gov^t	D°
5. John McKenna	D°	D°	2d August	30th Aug. 1803	Left in Newgate in the City of Dublin, and executed at Thomas-street.	D°
6. John Killeen	D°	D°	31st July	D°	Left in Newgate in the City of Dublin, and executed at Thomas-street.	D°
7. Martin Burke	Rebellion	D°	D°	D°	Left in Newgate in the City of Dublin.	D°
8. Michael Curran	D°	D°	D°	31st Oct. 1803	Discharged by order of Gov^t	D°
9. Felix O'Rourke	D°	D°	8th August	30th Aug. 1803	Sent to Newgate, and executed at Rathcoole.	D°
10. Michael Mahaffy	D°	D°	9th Ditto	25th Oct. 1803	Discharged by order of Gov^t	D°
11. John Ryan	D°	D°	D°	D°	D°	D°
12. St John Mason	Treasonable Practices	D°	D°	In Confinement	- - - -	D°
13. Ross McCann	D°	D°	10th Aug. 1803	11 Aug. 1803	Discharged by order of Gov^t	D°
14. Anne Toath	D°	D°	13th D°	4th October	D°	D°
15. James Dunn	D°	D°	D°	1st Oct. 1803	Discharged by order of Gov^t	D°
16. John Dunn	D°	D°	D°	D°	D°	D°
17. Richard McNally	D°	D°	D°	14th Jan. 1804	D°	D°
18. John Lawless	D°	D°	D°	D°	D°	D°
19. Philip Long	D°	D°	D°	In Confinement	- - - -	D°
20. Thomas Ridgeway	D°	D°	18th D°	18th Jan. 1804	Discharged by order of Gov^t	D°
21. Joseph Doran	High Treason	D°	23d D°	9th Sept. 1803	Discharged by order of the Commission Court.	D°
22. James Dixon	Treasonable Practices	D°	24th D°	11th Nov. 1804	Discharged by order of Gov^t	D°
23. Robert Emmett	High Treason	D°	26th D°	20th September	Executed at Thomas-street.	D°
24. Thomas Peppard	Treasonable Practices	D°	D°	In Confinement	- - - -	D°
25. John Hickson	D°	D°	28th D°	D°	- - - -	D°
26. Wm. Annesly Holton	High Treason	D°	2d September	D°	- - - -	D°
27. Judith Develin	Rebellion	D°	30th August	21st Jan. 1804	Discharged by order of Gov^t	D°
28. Mary Develin	D°	D°	D°	25th December	D°	D°
29. Thomas Duffy	D°	D°	2d September	21st D°	D°	D°
30. Michael McDonough	D°	D°	D°	17th November	D°	D°
31. Jane Rielly	Treasonable Practices	D°	D°	28th January	D°	D°
32. Anne Develin	D°	D°	3d September	In Confinement.	- - - -	D°
33. Bryan Develin	D°	D°	D°	D°	- - - -	D°
34. Winefred Develin	D°	D°	D°	21st Jan. 1804	Discharged by order of Gov^t	D°
35. Timothy Daly	D°	D°	7th D°	10th Dec. 1803	D°	D°
36. John Devine	D°	D°	D°	14th November	D°	D°
37. Thomas Keogh	High Treason.	D°	11th D°	6th December	D°	D°

'A return of persons'
in Kilmainham Gaol
(*House of Commons*, 1805, VI, p. 99).

A CALENDAR of PERSONS committed for High Treafon and Treafonable Practices to the Gaol of NEWGATE, in the Years 1803 and 1804.

NAMES of PRISONERS.	CHARGES against them, as expreffed in the Warrant.	Whether the Informations were on Oath, as ftated in the Warrant.	Length of TIME in Cuftody.	HOW DISPOSED OF.	FUNDS by which Maintained during Confinement.
N°					
1. John Ruffel - - -	High Treafon, and being concerned in the Rebellion now exifting in Ireland.	Not fpecified	From 28th July 1803 to 26th Septr 1803	Difcharged by Government	Government Allowance.
2. John Troy - - - -	D°	D°	D°	D°	D°
3. John Hart - - - -	D°	D°	D°	D°	D°
4. John Killen - - -	High Treafon, and for aiding, affifting, and abetting in the prefent Rebellion now exifting in Ireland.	D°	30th Aug. to 12th Sept. 1803	Executed	D°
5. Juo McKan alo McKenna	High Treafon, in furtherance of the Rebellion now exifting in Ireland.	D°	D°	D°	D°
6. Phelix Rourke - -	D°	Oath	D° to 10th D°	D°	D°
7. Hugh Fergufon - -	Sufpicious Perfons	Not fpecified	15th D° to 26th D°	Difcharged by Government	Gaol D°
8. John Mafterfon - -	D°	D°	D°	D°	D°
9. Laues Begly or Bayly -	High Treafon	Oath	20th D° to 10th March 1805	In Cuftody	D°
10. Michl Kelly - - -	D°	D°	D° to 17th Sept. 1803	Executed.	Government Allowance.
11. Thos Donnelly - - -	D°	D°	D° to	D° in Palmerftown.	D°
12. Nichs Farrell or Tyrrell	D°	D°	D°	D°	D°
13. Jas Byrne - - - -	D°	D°	D° to 4th D°	Executed	D°
14. Thos Maxwell Roche	D°	D°	D° to 2d D°	D°	D°
15. Edwd Kearney - - -	D°	D°	D° to 1ft D°	D°	D°
16. John Begg - - - -	D°	D°	D° to 17th D°	D°	D°
17. Walter Clare - - -	D°	D°	D° to March 10th 1805	In Cuftody.	Gaol D°
18. Owen Kirwan - - -	D°	D°	24th D° to Sept. 3d 1803	Executed.	Government D°
19. Bernard Coile - - -	Treafonable Practices	Not fpecified	D° to May 23d 1804	Tranfmitted to Kilmainham	D°
20. Dens Lambert Redmond	High Treafon	D°	27th D° to Oct. 5th D°	Executed.	D°
21. Mary Parkinfon - -	Having concealed Arms.	D°	16th D° to 4th Nov. 1803	Difcharged by Crown Solicitor	Gaol D°
22. Elinor Shelvey - - -	Treafonable Expreffions	D°	1ft Sept. to 11th Oct.	Tried and acquitted.	D°
23. Jno McDermott - -	High Treafon.	Oath	3d D° to 17th Sept.	Executed.	Government Allowance.
24. Jno Hayes or Hay - -	D°	D°	D°	D°	D°
25. Henry Howley - - -	D°	D°	17th to 28th D°	D°	Gaol D°
26. John McIntofh - - -	D°	D°	22d D° to 7th Oct.	D°	Government D°
27. Thomas Keenan - -	D°	D°	D°	D°	D°
28. Bryan Rourke - - -	Sufpicion of being guilty of High Treafon	Not fpecified	29th July to May 23d 1804	Tranfmitted to Kilmainham	D°
29. Patrick Marlay - - -	D°	D°	1ft Aug. to D°	D°	D°
30. Park Maguire - - -	D°	D°	19th D° to D°	D°	D°
31. Bryan Duigenan - -	D°	D°	24th D° to May 21ft	Difcharged by Government	D°
32. Bryan Kelch - - -	D°	D°	Aug. 31ft to May 21ft	D°	D°
33. Martin Burke - - -	D³	D°	30th to 23d D°	Tranfmitted to Kilmainham	D°
34. John Toole - - - -	D°	D°	Septr 11th to May 21ft	Difcharged by Government	D°
35. Henry Rofe - - -	Seditious Expreffions	Oath.	Nov. 25th to Dec. 6th	D° Time of Imprifonment out	Gaol D°
36. Edwd Kennedy - -	Having been guilty of Treafonable Practices.	Not fpecified	Nov. 4th to May 23d	Tranfmitted to Kilmainham	Government D°
37. John Flinn - - - -	High Treafon	D°	Dec. 31ft to May 21ft	Difcharged by Government	D°
38. John Reilly - - - -	Treafonable Practices	D°	March 10th 1804 to D°	D°	D°

'A calendar of persons committed for High Treason…' in Newgate Gaol

(*House of Commons*, 1805, VI, p. 103).

The suspension of *habeas corpus* and imposition of martial law enabled state agents to detain thousands of subjects across the country. Those brought to trial were concentrated in Newgate to facilitate their appearance in the adjacent Green Street Courthouse.

107

Major H.C. Sirr **by J. Martyn** (NLI, EP SIRR-HE (1) I).

Town Major Henry Charles Sirr, an ex-army officer and Dublin's *de facto* chief of police, was the most effective counter-insurgent of his generation. Sirr arrested Lord Edward Fitzgerald in May 1798 and monitored the United Irish committees that met in the capital. He also handled secret service bounties and ran a small staff of turned United Irishmen based in the Castle.

House at Harold's Cross, Dublin, where Robert Emmet was captured by Major Sirr (private collection).

Emmet lived quietly in the Palmer home off Mount Drummond Avenue, Harold's Cross, until 25 August, when Sirr and an assistant called to check the identities of the occupants. Among the papers seized was Emmet's manuscript copy of a sermon that influenced the tenor and structure of his trial speech.

this was found by Major [illegible] Henry [illegible]
in [illegible] lodgings Harolds cross

y mount, interceeding with his incensed Father,
r the redemption of y world; & with such earnest
mportunity, with such strong crying and tears,
refsing his requests, that in this convulsive agony
s pang of devotion, his soul is said to be exceeding
rrowful, even unto death; to be surrounded with
rief, and cast into such violent consternation, as to †
hen all y pores of his body, & tho' it was night, cold
ight, & amid y fall of chilling dews, he sweat, — sweat
lood, † sweat great drops of blood, running down
n reeking streams to y ground. Whilst he is thus la-
ouring for our salvation, see him betray'd by one of his
wn disciples into y hands of those ungrateful Jews, who
ad been fed with his miracles, healed by his touch,
ispofsefs'd with his voice, and instructed with his
octrine; and against whom he might have command-
d down legions of angels to his rescue and their
estruction! Yet when he might have struck them
the ground, by the very majesty of his look, in-
tead of taking vengeance on them, he salutes the
ery traitor by the name of friend, and works a
iracle to cure the wounded ear of one of his af-
fsins. Well might he have said, for which of my
ood deeds are ye come out with swords & staves,
s against a theif to take me?
2ᵈˡʸ From the mount, let us next attend him

Sermon on the Mount
(NLI, LO 1,047).

The Arrest of Robert Emmet by Major Sirr, at Harold's Cross, Dublin, August 25th, 1803, **J.D. Reigh** (*Shamrock*, 15 March 1890).

Sirr was obliged to open fire on Emmet and give chase across a number of gardens before the fugitive was apprehended.

No.	Names	When Committed	By Whom	Crimes
89	James Dixon	24th August 1803	Secretary Wickham	Treasonable Practices
90	Robert Emmet	26th August 1803	Secretary Wickham	High Treason
91	John Hickson	20th August 1803	Secretary Wickham	Treasonable Practices
92	Wm Annesley Houlton	2d September 1803	Secretary Wickham	High Treason
93	Judith Develine	30th August 1803	Town Major Genl	Rebellion

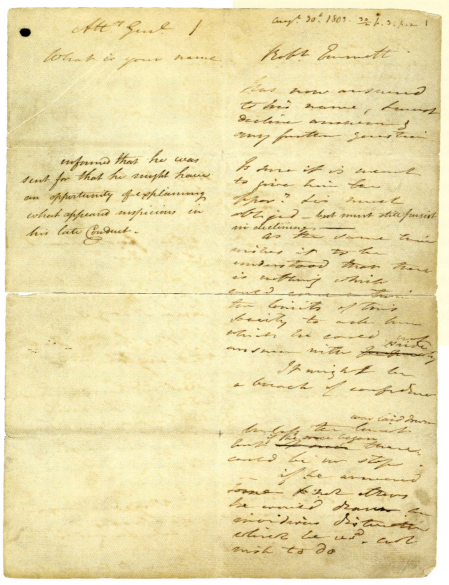

Examination of Emmet (NAI, Rebellion Papers, 620/11/132).

Emmet was interviewed in Dublin Castle by members of the Privy Council on 30 August 1803 but refused to cooperate with his captors.

Discharged & By Whom | Place of abode | Remarks
... Gov.t 11 Nov.r 1804 | Kilmainham |
... Thomas Street 20th Sep.t 1803 | Dublin | Tried before Lord Norbury &c 19th Sep.t 1803 Guilty
 | Dublin | ... by ... Esq for the order of Government 12th Aug.t 1805
 | Dublin |
... by Alex.r Marsden Esq.r 21st Jan.y 1804 | C.o Dublin |

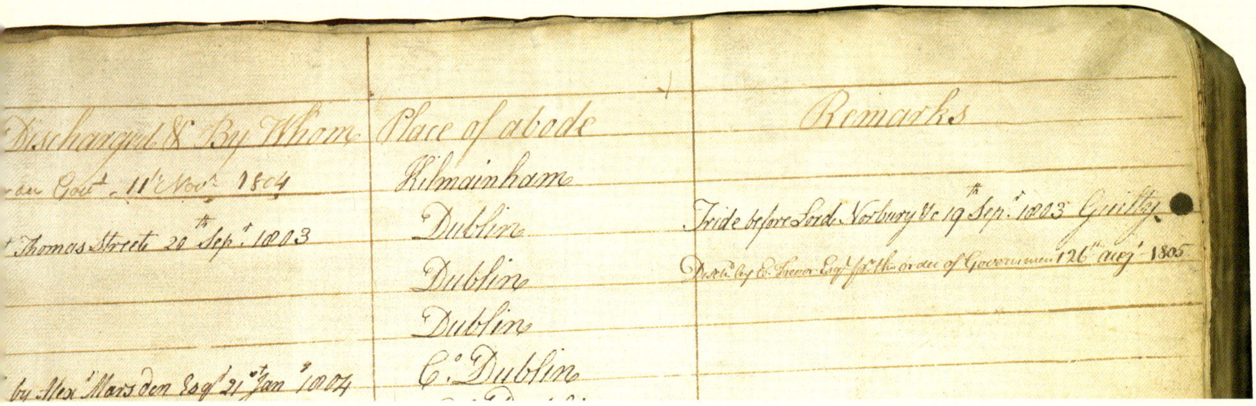

Kilmainham Gaol register 1798–1814 (NAI).

Dom.k Doyle Deputy Gaoler of Newgate his Account for Dieting the Sev.l State Prisoners after named pursuant to Mr. Marsden's Directions communicated to him by the Letter of Mr. Archer

1803		£	s	d
Sep.t 7	To Walter Clare his Diet to the 15th Oct.r – 39 days at 3/3 p day – still living	6	6	9
	To Laurence Bayly's his d.o to d.o – d.o days – at d.o – still d.o	6	6	9
	To John Beggs his d.o – to the 16th Sept.r – 10 days at d.o	1	12	6
	To Felix O'Rourke his d.o – to the 10 d.o – 3 d.o – at d.o Inclusive	"	9	9
	To John McKenna's his d.o – to the 11th d.o – 5 d.o at d.o – d.o	"	16	3
	To John Kiln his d.o – to – d.o – d.o – d.o – d.o	"	16	3
	To Michael Kelly his d.o – to the 14th d.o 7 d.o – d.o – d.o	1	2	9
	To Nicholas Tyrell his d.o – to d.o – d.o – d.o – d.o	1	2	9
	To Thos. Donnelly his d.o – to d.o – d.o – d.o – d.o	1	2	9
	To John Hayes his d.o – to 11th d.o – 5 d.o – d.o – d.o	0	16	3
⊕→	To Robt. Emmett Esq.re one days Diet	"	3	3
	To Henry Howley's Diet to the 17th d.o – 11 d.o – d.o – at d.o	1	15	9
	To John McIntosh's d.o – to the 18th d.o – 12 d.o – d.o – at d.o	1	19	0
	To Thos. Keenan's d.o – to the 20th d.o – 14 d.o – d.o – at d.o	2	5	6
	To John Russell's, John Troy's, Bernard Coyle's, & John Hart's Diet, one Week each 28 days, at 3/3 p day	4	11	0
	To Denis Lambert Redmond his d.o to the 6th of Oct.r last 30 days at 3/3 p day	4	17	6
	To one pint Wine ordered him daily by the Surgeons at 1/7½	2	8	9
	To 3 Quarts of Whey daily – 90 Quarts at 4d p Quart	1	10	0
	To 30 days Diet to the Surgeons Assistant who attended him at 3/3 p day	4	17	6
	To d.o – d.o – d.o to two Men Fox & Mulloy who attended him Night & day at 3/3 p day each	9	15	0
	To 30 gallons Malt Liquor each Night for them at 1/2 p Gall.	1	15	0
	To Candles at 4d p Night	"	10	0
	Errors Excepted £	57	1	0
	To Dominick Doyle's Extraordinary Diligence, and Care in watching Redmond, at various times of the Night, and the above named Prisoners	11	7	6
		68	8	6

Received the above Sum of Sixty Eight Pounds ... from ... 26 Nov.r 1803
Dom.k Doyle

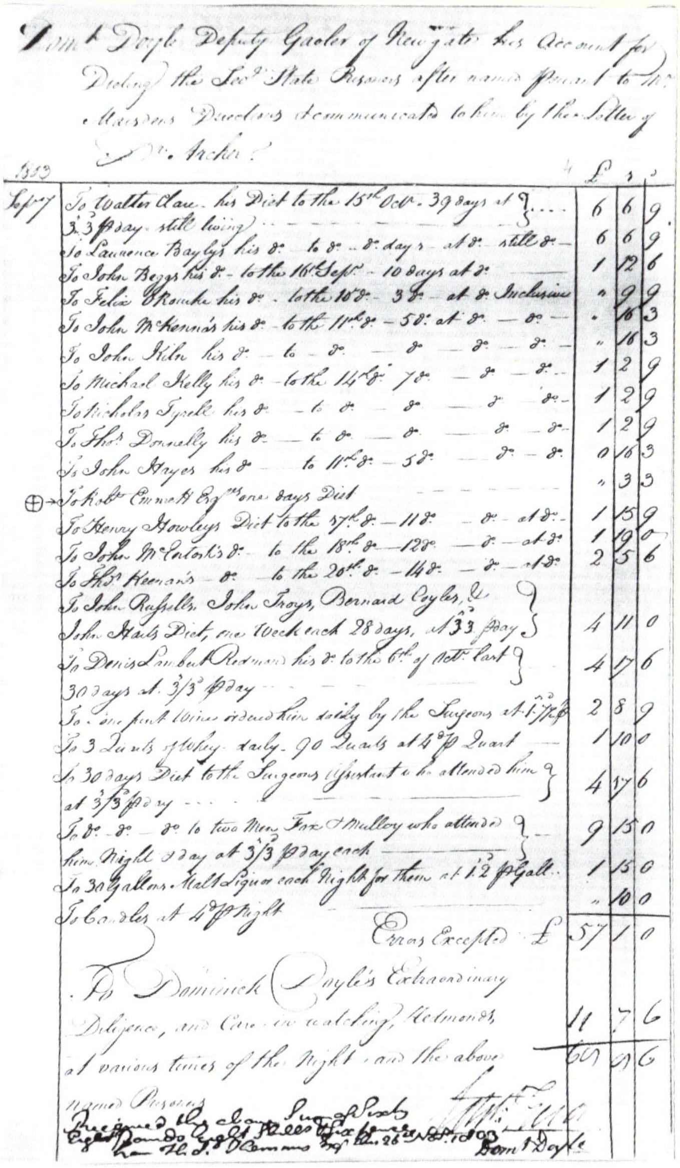

Emmet in Newgate (Dúchas/Emmet family).

Emmet was sent from the Castle to Kilmainham Gaol on 30 August to await trial. He was accommodated in a comparatively spacious, ground-floor reception room. When required to attend the Special Commission in Green Street, Emmet was temporarily confined in the more convenient Newgate. He busied himself writing letters, including several smuggled out to Sarah Curran. Most of those listed in gaoler Dominic Doyle's accounts were executed.

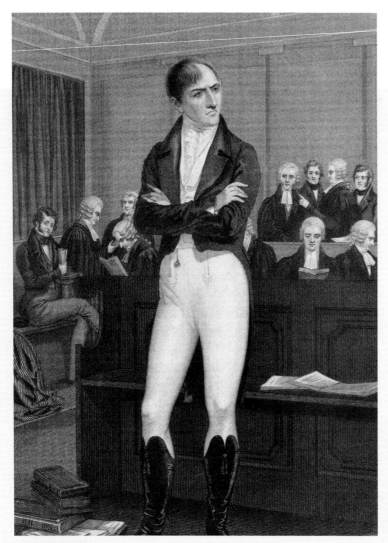

The unfortunate Mr. Rob[er]t Emmett [sic]
(*Walker's Hibernian Magazine*, September 1803).

Robert Emmett [sic], engraved by William Read (NLI, PD EMME-RO (10) II).

The trial commenced on the morning of 19 September 1803 and lasted for over twelve hours.

Two lawyers at the Trial of Robert Emmet... by James Petrie
(NGI, 7885).

James Petrie, a suspected United Irishman and ex-political prisoner, attended Emmet's trial and drew the defendant on the back of an envelope and other loose papers. This work formed the basis of a portrait obtained by Sir Jonah Barrington and produced the best frontal image of the Dubliner. Petrie subsequently engraved a left profile of Emmet.

Untitled sketch of Emmet by James Petrie (Emmet, *Memoir*).

115

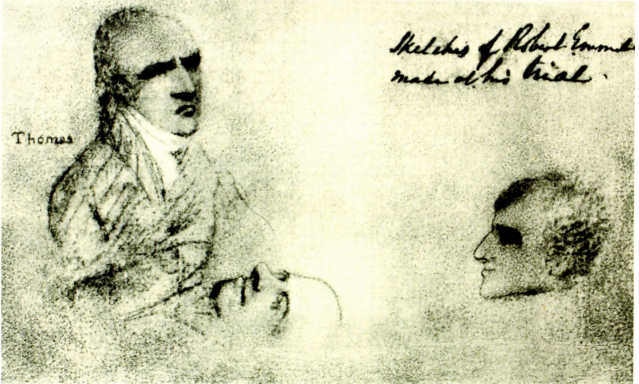

Untitled sketch of Emmet by James Petrie (Dúchas/Emmet family).

***Rob.[ert] Emmet Esq.* drawn and engraved by Henry Brocas, Snr** (NLI, PD 2129 (TX) 8).

***The trial of Robert Emmet* by James Petrie** (NGI, 7886).

Wexford engraver Henry Brocas, Snr, was commissioned by Dublin Castle to sketch Emmet in court (see opposite). This irregular step was taken to increase the impact of the government's propaganda offensive. A traditional left profile version was offered for sale, whereas a simplified form was used in an anti-French broadside.

The drawing opposite shows Emmet descending from the dock after delivering his famous speech. It has been attributed to a Mrs Orr, a niece of one of the trial judges.

Within image 1:
If the FRENCH land in Ireland, Oh, my Countrymen, meet them on the Shore with a Torch in one hand — a Sword in the other — receive them with all the destruction of War — Immolate them in their Boats before our Native Soil should be polluted by a Foreign Foe.

Memoirs of Mr. Emmet by Henry Brocas, Snr (NLI, PD 2129 (TX) 9).

Robert Emmet in the dock (NLI, 3002 (TX)).

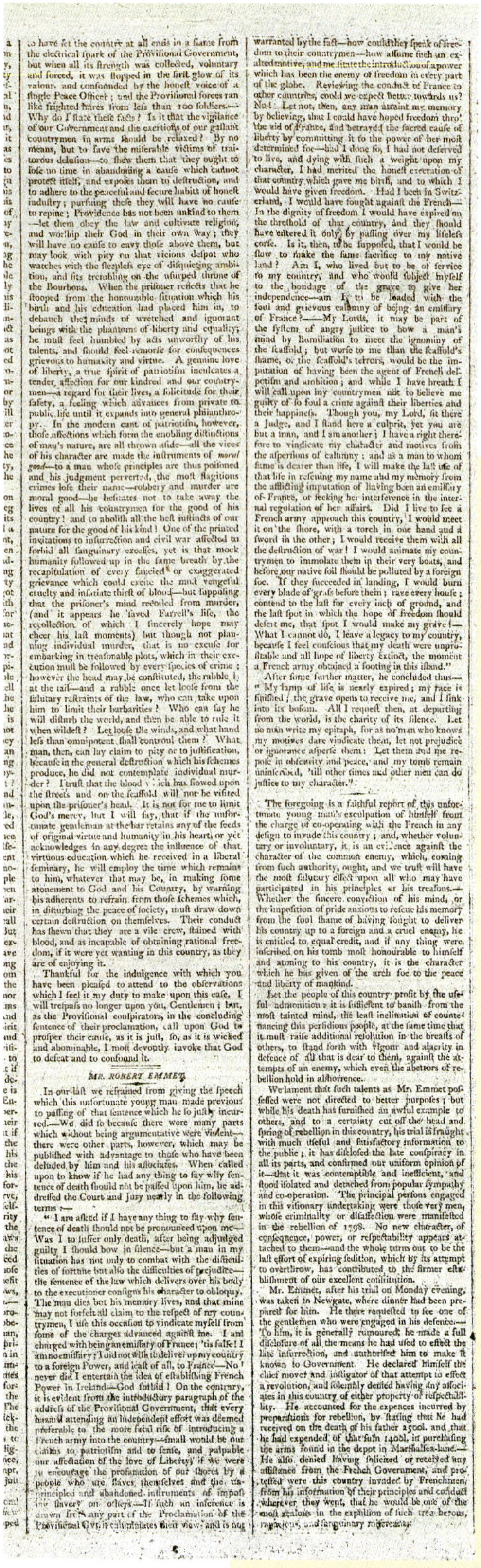

to have set the country at all ends in a flame from the electrical spark of the Provisional Government, but when all its strength was collected, voluntary and forced, it was stopped in the first glow of its valour, and confounded by the honest voice of a single Peace Officer; and the Provisional forces ran like frighted hares from less than 100 soldiers.—Why do I state these facts? Is it that the vigilance of our Government and the exertions of our gallant countrymen in arms should be relaxed? By no means, but to save the miserable victims of traitorous delusion—to shew them that they ought to lose no time in abandoning a cause which cannot protect itself, and exposes them to destruction, and to adhere to the peaceful and secure habits of honest industry; pursuing these they will have no cause to repine; Providence has not been unkind to them—let them obey the law and cultivate religion, and worship their God in their own way; they will have no cause to envy those above them, but may look with pity on that vicious despot who watches with the sleepless eye of disquieting ambition, and sits trembling on the usurped throne of the Bourbons. When the prisoner reflects that he stooped from the honourable situation which his birth and his education had placed him in, to debauch the minds of wretched and ignorant beings with the phantoms of liberty and equality, he must feel humbled by acts unworthy of his talents, and should feel remorse for consequences grievous to humanity and virtue. A genuine love of liberty, a true spirit of patriotism inculcates a tender affection for our kindred and our countrymen—a regard for their lives, a solicitude for their safety, a feeling which advances from private to public life until it expands into general philanthropy. In the modern cant of patriotism, however, those affections which form the enobling distinctions of man's nature, are all thrown aside—all the vices of his character are made the instruments of *moral good*—to a man whose principles are thus poisoned and his judgment perverted, the most flagitious crimes lose their name—robbery and murder are moral good—he hesitates not to take away the lives of all his countrymen for the good of his country! and to abolish all the best instincts of our nature for the good of his kind! One of the printed invitations to insurrection and civil war affected to forbid all sanguinary excesses, yet is that mock humanity followed up in the same breath by the recapitulation of every fancied or exaggerated grievance which could excite the most vengeful cruelty and insatiate thirst of blood—but supposing that the prisoner's mind recoiled from murder, (and it appears he saved Farrell's life, the recollection of which I sincerely hope may cheer his last moments) but though not planning individual murder, that is no excuse for embarking in treasonable plots, which in their execution must be followed by every species of crime; however the head may be constituted, the rabble is at the tail—and a rabble once let loose from the salutary restraints of the law, who can take upon him to limit their barbarities? Who can say he will disturb the world, and then be able to rule it when wildest? Let loose the winds, and what hand less than omnipotent shall controul them? What man, then, can lay claim to pity or to justification, because in the general destruction which his schemes produce, he did not contemplate individual murder? I trust that the blood which has flowed upon the streets and on the scaffold will not be visited upon the prisoner's head. It is not for me to limit God's mercy, but I will say, that if the unfortunate gentleman at the bar retains any of the seeds of original virtue and humanity in his heart, or yet acknowledges in any degree the influence of that virtuous education which he received in a liberal seminary, he will employ the time which remains to him, whatever that may be, in making some atonement to God and his Country, by warning his adherents to refrain from those schemes which, in disturbing the peace of society, must draw down certain destruction on themselves. Their conduct has shewn that they are a vile crew, stained with blood, and as incapable of obtaining rational freedom, if it were yet wanting in this country, as they are of enjoying it.

Thankful for the indulgence with which you have been pleased to attend to the observations which I feel it my duty to make upon this case, I will trespass no longer upon you, Gentlemen; but, as the Provisional conspirators, in the concluding sentence of their proclamation, call upon God to prosper their cause, as it is just, so, as it is wicked and abominable, I most devoutly invoke that God to defeat and to confound it.

MR. ROBERT EMMET.

In our last we refrained from giving the speech which this unfortunate young man made previous to passing of that sentence which he so justly incurred.—We did so because there were many parts which without being argumentative were violent—there were other parts, however, which may be published with advantage to those who have been deluded by him and his associates. When called upon to know if he had any thing to say why sentence of death should not be passed upon him, he addressed the Court and Jury nearly in the following terms:—

"I am asked if I have any thing to say why sentence of death should not be pronounced upon me—Was I to suffer only death, after being adjudged guilty I should bow in silence—but a man in my situation has not only to combat with the difficulties of fortune but also the difficulties of prejudice—the sentence of the law which delivers over his body to the executioner consigns his character to obloquy. The man dies but his memory lives, and that mine may not forfeit all claim to the respect of my countrymen, I use this occasion to vindicate myself from some of the charges advanced against me. I am charged with being an emissary of France; 'tis false! I am no emissary; I did not wish to deliver up my country to a foreign Power, and least of all, to France—No! never did I entertain the idea of establishing French Power in Ireland—God forbid! On the contrary, it is evident from the introductory paragraph of the address of the Provisional Government, that every hazard attending an independent effort was deemed preferable to the more fatal risk of introducing a French army into the country—small would be our claims to patriotism and to sense, and palpable our affectation of the love of Liberty, if we were to encourage the profanation of our shores by a people who are slaves themselves and the unprincipled and abandoned instruments of imposing slavery on others.—If such an inference is drawn from any part of the Proclamation of the Provisional Gvt. it calumniates their views, and is not warranted by the fact—how could they speak of freedom to their countrymen—how assume such an exalted motive, and meditate the introduction of a power which has been the enemy of freedom in every part of the globe. Reviewing the conduct of France to other countries, could we expect better towards us? No! Let not, then, any man attaint my memory by believing, that I could have hoped freedom thro' the aid of France, and betrayed the sacred cause of liberty by committing it to the power of her most determined foe—had I done so, I had not deserved to live, and dying with such a weight upon my character, I had merited the honest execration of that country which gave me birth, and to which I would have given freedom. Had I been in Switzerland, I would have fought against the French—In the dignity of freedom I would have expired on the threshold of that country, and they should have entered it only by passing over my lifeless corse. Is it, then, to be supposed, that I would be slow to make the same sacrifice to my native land? Am I, who lived but to be of service to my country, and who would subject myself to the bondage of the grave to give her independence—am I to be loaded with the foul and grievous calumny of being an emissary of France?——My Lords, it may be part of the system of angry justice to bow a man's mind by humiliation to meet the ignominy of the scaffold; but worse to me than the scaffold's shame, or the scaffold's terrors, would be the imputation of having been the agent of French despotism and ambition; and while I have breath I will call upon my countrymen not to believe me guilty of so foul a crime against their liberties and their happiness. Though you, my Lord, sit there a Judge, and I stand here a culprit, yet you are but a man, and I am another; I have a right therefore to vindicate my character and motives from the aspersions of calumny; and as a man to whom fame is dearer than life, I will make the last use of that life in rescuing my name and my memory from the afflicting imputation of having been an emissary of France, or seeking her interference in the internal regulation of her affairs. Did I live to see a French army approach this country, I would meet it on the shore, with a torch in one hand and a sword in the other; I would receive them with all the destruction of war! I would animate my countrymen to immolate them in their very boats, and before our native soil should be polluted by a foreign foe. If they succeeded in landing, I would burn every blade of grass before them; raze every house; contend to the last for every inch of ground, and the last spot in which the hope of freedom should desert me, that spot I would make my grave!—What I cannot do, I leave a legacy to my country, because I feel conscious that my death were unprofitable and all hope of liberty extinct, the moment a French army obtained a footing in this island."

After some further matter, he concluded thus—"My lamp of life is nearly expired; my race is finished; the grave opens to receive me, and I sink into its bosom. All I request then, at departing from the world, is the charity of its silence. Let no man write my epitaph, for as no man who knows my motives dare vindicate them, let not prejudice or ignorance asperse them: Let them and me repose in obscurity and peace, and my tomb remain uninscribed, 'till other times and other men can do justice to my character."

The foregoing is a faithful report of this unfortunate young man's exculpation of himself from the charge of co-operating with the French in any design to invade this country; and, whether voluntary or involuntary, it is an evidence against the character of the common enemy, which, coming from such authority, ought, and we trust will have the most salutary effect upon all who may have participated in his principles or his treasons.—Whether the sincere conviction of his mind, or the imposition of pride anxious to rescue his memory from the foul shame of having sought to deliver his country up to a foreign and a cruel enemy, he is entitled to equal credit, and if any thing were inscribed on his tomb most honourable to himself and atoning to his country, it is the character which he has given of the arch foe to the peace and liberty of mankind.

Let the people of this country profit by the useful admonition: it is sufficient to banish from the most tainted mind, the least inclination of countenancing this perfidious people, at the same time that it must raise additional resolution in the breasts of others, to stand forth with vigour and alacrity in defence of all that is dear to them, against the attempts of an enemy, which even the abettors of rebellion hold in abhorrence.

We lament that such talents as Mr. Emmet possessed were not directed to better purposes; but while his death has furnished an awful example to others, and to a certainty cut off the head and spring of rebellion in this country, his trial is fraught with much useful and satisfactory information to the public; it has disclosed the late conspiracy in all its parts, and confirmed our uniform opinion of it—that it was contemptible and inefficient, and stood isolated and detached from popular sympathy and co-operation. The principal persons engaged in this visionary undertaking were those very men, whose criminality or disaffection were manifested in the rebellion of 1798. No new character, of consequence, power, or respectability appears attached to them—and the whole turns out to be the last effort of expiring sedition, which by its attempt to overthrow, has contributed to the firmer establishment of our excellent constitution.

Mr. Emmet, after his trial on Monday evening, was taken to Newgate, where dinner had been prepared for him. He there requested to see one of the gentlemen who were engaged in his defence.—To him, it is generally rumoured, he made a full disclosure of all the means he had used to effect the late insurrection, and authorised him to make it known to Government. He declared himself the chief mover and instigator of that attempt to effect a revolution, and solemnly denied having any associates in this country of either property or respectability. He accounted for the expences incurred by preparations for rebellion, by stating that he had received on the death of his father 2500l. and that he had expended of that sum 1400l. in purchasing the arms found in the depot in Marshalsea-lane.—He also denied having solicited or received any assistance from the French Government, and protested were this country invaded by Frenchmen, from his information of their principles and conduct wherever they went, that he would be one of the most zealous in the expulsion of such treacherous, rapacious, and sanguinary miscreants.

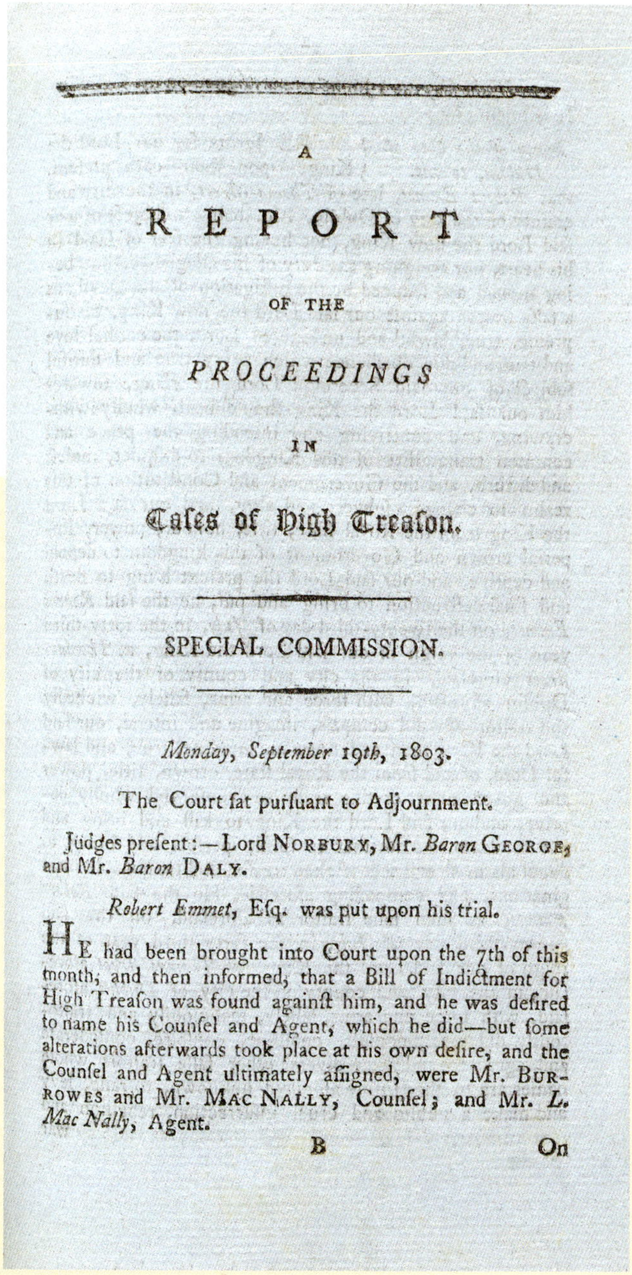

A

REPORT

OF THE

PROCEEDINGS

IN

Cases of High Treason.

SPECIAL COMMISSION.

Monday, September 19th, 1803.

The Court sat pursuant to Adjournment.

Judges present:—Lord NORBURY, Mr. *Baron* GEORGE, and Mr. *Baron* DALY.

Robert Emmet, Esq. was put upon his trial.

HE had been brought into Court upon the 7th of this month, and then informed, that a Bill of Indictment for High Treason was found against him, and he was desired to name his Counsel and Agent, which he did—but some alterations afterwards took place at his own desire, and the Counsel and Agent ultimately assigned, were Mr. BURROWES and Mr. MAC NALLY, Counsel; and Mr. *L. Mac Nally*, Agent.

B On

William Ridgeway, *A report of the trial of Robert Emmet, upon an indictment for high treason* (Dublin, 1803).

Speech from the dock

(*Dublin Evening Post*, 22 September 1803).

THE TRIAL
AND
DYING BEHAVIOUR
OF
Mr R. Emmett,

Who was Executed September the 20th, for High Treason.—Together with his Solemn Exhortation to his Countrymen to reject the proffered Friendship and Assistance of Despotic, Cruel, and Perfidious FRANCE.

ON Monday September 19, ROBERT EMMETT was put to the bar, at Dublin, on trial for High Treason. The prisoner challenged nineteen peremptorily out of the pannel for a Petit Jury, and six were set aside by the Crown.

The Attorney General took a retrospective view of the public calamities incident to the spirit of insurrection which had hitherto prevaded the minds of the common people of that country.

The prisoner at the bar, if Mr. Attorney was properly instructed, would appear by substantial evidence, together with a variety of corroborating circumstances, to have been the prime source, origin, and spirit of the recent insurrection in this city, so enormously wicked in the conception, but so truly contemptible and puerile both in the plan and execution.

The prisoner in a speech marked by some traits of ingenuity and elocution, justified the conduct imputed to him, on firm and long adopted principles.

The Jury returned a verdict GUILTY, without leaving the box; and Lord Norbury pronounced sentence of DEATH on him.

At ten o'clock this morning, (Sept. 20), a confidential friend of this unfortunate Gentleman was permitted to visit him at Kilmainham gaol. The visitor, a professional Gentleman of considerable eminence, on his entrance into the culprit's chamber found him reading the Litany in the service of the Church of England in the presence of the Rev. Mr. Gamble, the Ordinary of Newgate; after which he made a hearty breakfast. Retiring afterwards to a room with his friend, after certain family communications, he adverted to the circumstance of having his pockets examined in the dock on the preceding evening, for some instrument with which it was apprehended he might destroy himself. He disclaimed such notion, alledging it was incompatible with the religion he professed.

The culprit was led from Kilmainham gaol under a strong military guard, composed of detachments both of Cavalry and Infantry of the Regular Troops quartered at the Barracks. He arrived about three o'clock at the temporary gallows, in Thomas-street, in a carriage with two clergy-men. In his progress thither his demeanour, however, did not appear of that serious cast befitting the awfulness of his situation, or the religious sentiments he had uttered in the morning. He gazed about, particularly in Dirty-lane, the scene of his exploits, with a species of light inattentive smile, approaching a laugh, until he was carried to the place of execution, and spoke and nodded to some of his acquaintance with the greatest coolness. After mounting the platform attached to the gallows, he addressed the surrounding crowd in a few words, saying he died in peace and universal love and kindness with all mankind. While the Executioner was adjusting the rope round his neck, he became very pale, and he seemed earnestly to talk and expostulate with him most probably about some awkwardness in his manner, from which he felt an inconvenience. After the hangman had pulled a cap over his eyes, the culprit put up his hands, pinioned as they were, and partly removed it. The platform was dextrously removed. After which he hung for near a minute quite motionless, but violent convulsions then seized him, which lasted for several minutes. The process of beheading, &c. was afterwards gone through, and his body removed to Newgate.

The admirable description which he drew of the French fraternity must powerfully operate on that part of the people of Ireland, who seek, through the agency of the First Consul to disunite these countries.

"I have," said he, "been accused of being actuated by a wish to bring about a revolution of this country, through the means of French influence. I deny that either myself or the Provisional Government, had any such idea in contemplation. Our own resources were sufficient to accomplish the object. As to French interposition, it cannot be too much deprecated; and I exhort the people of Ireland to beware of such assistance. I urge them in the strongest manner to burn their houses—nay even the very grass on which a Frenchman shall land. Various opportunities have occured to me of witnessing the misery and desolation they have produced in every country where they have gained an entrance, under the fallacious pretences of aiding the Inhabitants who considered themselves in a state of oppression."

Jennings & Co, Printers, Upper Mary'lane &

119

The trial and dying behaviour of Mr. R. Emmett [sic] (Emmet, *Memoir*).

The government moved quickly to reduce the impact of Emmet's speech by selectively quoting and otherwise misrepresenting his opinions on the French alliance.

The trial of Robert Emmet, September 19th, 1803 by J.D.R.[eigh] (*Shamrock*, December 1892).

Facing page
The trial of Robert Emmet. Born at Dublin in 1778, Died September 20, 1803 (NLI, EP EMME-RO (19) IV).

Emmet's stoicism in court and stirring speech from the dock ensured his iconic status among nationalists.

Newgate Gaol by Robert Pool, engraved by John Lodge (NLI, IR 914133).

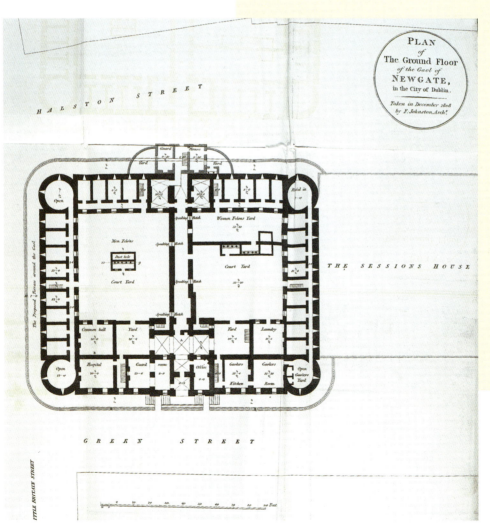

Plan of Newgate (*Parliamentary Papers*, 1809).

After sentencing, Emmet was returned to Newgate, where Revd Thomas Gamble, prison chaplain and acquaintance, found him in good spirits. He was heavily ironed until moved later that night to Kilmainham.

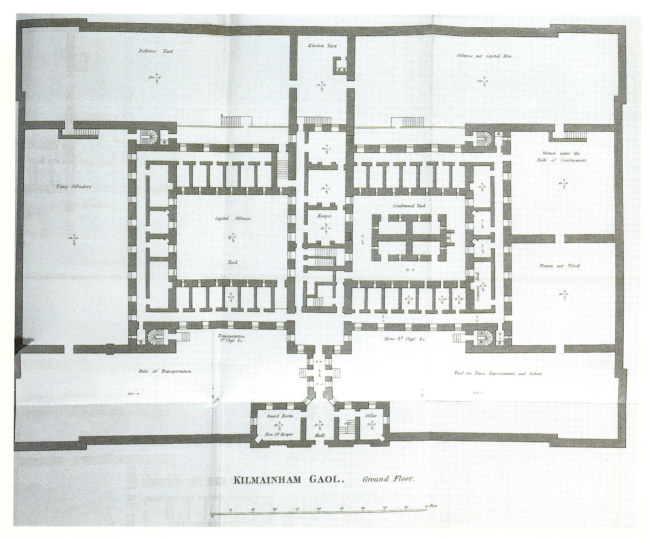

Plan of Kilmainham (*Parliamentary Papers*, 1809).

Emmet spent the last night of his life in Kilmainham drafting political documents, drawing and writing letters to friends and family members. His plight moved the Roscommon Militiamen on guard duty.

I find I have but a few hours to live but if it was the
last moment & that the power of utterance was leaving me I would thank you from
the bottom of my heart for your generous expressions of affection & forgiveness to me

God bless you my dearest Ric'd I am obliged to
leave off immediately— Rob't Emmet

Emmet's letter to Richard Curran (NLI, MS 8079 (3)).

Thomas Addis Emmet (Dúchas/Emmet family).

William Wickham (Dúchas/Emmet family).

Sept' 20. 1803

Had I been permitted to proceed with
...ication it was my intention not only to have acknowledge
...usay with which I feel with gratitude that I have been
...onally treated but also to have done the most public justice
...e mildness of the present administration of this country
...d at the same time to have acquitted them, as far as
...ted with me, of any charge of remisoness in not having
...viously detected a conspiracy which from its closeness
...now it was impossible to have done. I confess that I
...ould have preferred this mode if it had been permitted

Emmet's letter to Wickham, 20 September 1803 (Dúchas/Emmet family).

as it would thereby have enabled me to clear myself from an
imputation under which I might in consequence lie, and to
have stated why such an <u>administration</u> did not prevent,
but under the peculiar situation of this country, perhaps
rather accelerated my determination, to make an effort for
the overthrow of a <u>government</u> of which I do not think
equally highly. However as I have been deprived of that
opportunity I think it right now to make an acknowledgement
which Justice requires from me as a man, and which I do not
feel to be in the least derogatory from my decided principles
as an Irishman.

I have the honor to be
Sir
with the greatest respect your most Obedient
humble Servant

Robt Emmet

Emmet's last letters informed Richard Curran and Thomas Addis Emmet of his engagement to Sarah Curran. A final note of gratitude to Wickham undermined the Englishman's faith in his political career and hastened his retirement.

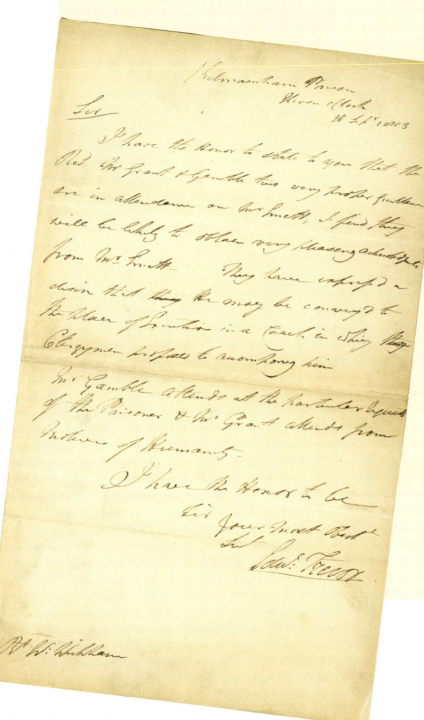

Dr Trevor to Marsden, 20 September 1803 (NAI, Rebellion Papers, 620/11/133).

Kilmainham's medical superintendent, Dr Edward Trevor, was largely responsible for thwarting Emmet's planned jailbreak on 5 September. Trevor permitted Revd Gamble to accompany Emmet to the scaffold in return for a report on the Dubliner's state of mind.

Robert Emmet on the scaffold (Kilmainham).

Overleaf

Variously attributed to F.W. Byrne of Ormond Terrace, Rathmines, or F. Byrne of Castle Avenue, Clontarf, this dramatic print of Emmet's execution was sold in Dublin in August 1877. While presented from a non-existent vantage, the view depicted accords with contemporary accounts of the execution.

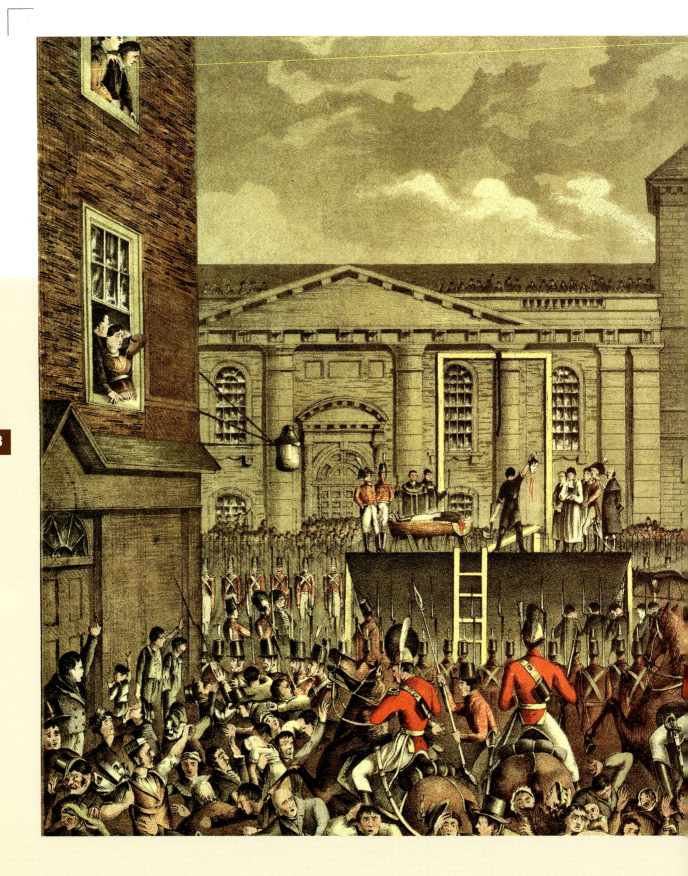

*Execution of Robert Emmet, in
Thomas Street, 20th September
1803* (NLI, PD HP (1803) 1). ↘

Butcher's block used by Thomas Galvin
(Kilmainham, photograph by Con Brogan).

Death mask of Robert Emmet (NGI, 11,166).

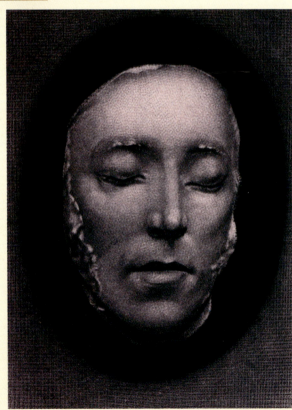

The decollation of Emmet by executioner Thomas Galvin took place on a deal block table procured from a local butcher. The block was displayed in public outside the Market House for a number of days. Emmet's body was left in view of his imprisoned associates in Kilmainham while Petrie cast a death mask.

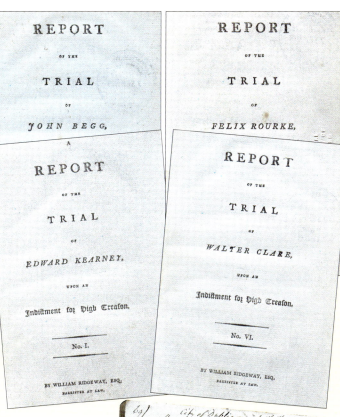

The Special Commission.

The Special Commission, convened in Green Street on 31 August 1803 to try suspected participants in the Rising of 1803, was highly selective in terms of those tried. Felix Rourke and Denis Lambert Redmond were the only two senior figures other than Emmet to appear in court in Dublin. While Henry Howley was a mid-level activist who had shot Colonel Lyde Brown and Castle Tower-Keeper John Hanlon, most of the remaining defendants were junior conspirators arrested in suspicious circumstances on the night of the Rising.

Crown Circuit Book of Judge Mathias Finucane (NLI, MS 5973, fols 69 and 70).

Judge Mathias Finucane joined a panel consisting of John Toler (Lord Norbury), St George Daly, William Downes and Baron Denis George in preparing the calendar of the Special Commission and trying those indicted for high treason. Finucane's personal notes reveal the perfunctory nature of this process.

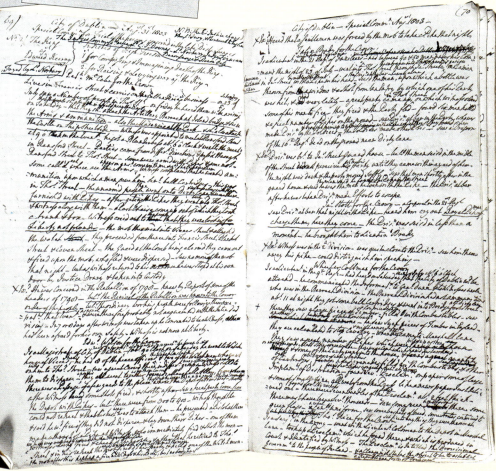

Arrest of Thomas Russell (*Walker's Hibernian Magazine*, 1803).

The seizure of Thomas Russell on Parliament Street on 9 September astounded those who believed that martial law had cowed the United Irishmen. Russell was transferred to the Special Commission at Downpatrick, Co. Down, where he had failed to mobilise a significant insurgent force on 23 July 1803. He was tried on 20 October and executed the following day. Russell's death resulted in the total dispersal of the coterie assembled by Emmet and Long.

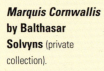

Marquis Cornwallis **by Balthasar Solvyns** (private collection).

RECEIVED *from Captain* Cash *of the*
Company of Rotunda Infantry, *the following Articles, viz.*

A Musket and Bayonet, complete,
A Pouch and Belt, Bayonet Belt, Scabbard and Musket Sling,
A Haversack and Canteen,
A Uniform Coatee, Breeches and Leggings, £3.1~½
A Uniform Cap and Feather.
Blue Pantaloons

All which, as a Yeoman of his Company, I engage to keep in a clean, Soldier-like manner, and to return the whole of them to my said Captain whenever I may called on for them, agreeable to the 5th Section of the Yeomanry Act of the 42d of George III.

Dublin, *14* Day of *August* 1803

Edward Dunn

recommended by Campbell.
N.º 33 Granby Row
ser.d with Ed Clarke Esq.r Palmerstown during last rebellion

Equipment list of the Rotunda Infantry (NLI, MS 9879).

The Rising accelerated an overdue reorganisation of the yeomanry, whose very existence had been threatened by the mooted Army of the Reserve.

The *Tellicherry*, an East Indiaman of similar design to the *Marquis Cornwallis*, sailed for New South Wales on 28 August 1805 with several important United Irishmen, not least Wicklow leaders Michael Dwyer, John Mernagh and Arthur Devlin. Their status as free men resulted from the Castle's desire to neutralise all remaining armed groups by a combination of coercion and clemency. The Dwyer circle exercised its right to obtain convict labour by selecting sentenced *Tellicherry* United Irishmen Walter Clare and Michael Maguire. Clare had been implicated in the Rising in Dublin, and Maguire, a former colonel of Down insurgents, was an associate of Thomas Russell.

Chapter 6

Remember Emmet

The restoration of *habeas corpus* in the spring of 1806, at the behest of the new Whig government of Charles James Fox and Lord Grenville, led to the release of the last state prisoners held in connection with the Rising of 1803. The ongoing war with France, however, and the censorious climate engendered by libel cases arising from published comments on Emmet's trial, militated against a mature reappraisal of what had occurred in Dublin, Kildare, Antrim and Down two years before. Most protagonists preferred to attribute the Rising to Emmet's leadership, not least Philip Long, who had survived the crackdown without implicating his friends. Two other key conspirators, Allen and Dowdall, were living in France, where the Napoleonic regime maintained its interest in campaigning in Ireland, a contingency all but voided by heavy naval losses sustained in October 1805 at Trafalgar. Walter Cox, the peripatetic gunsmith, propagandist and militant Republican, wrote a problematic, if supportive, biographical sketch of Emmet in his November 1808 edition of the *Irish Magazine*. Cox had led the Broadstone rebels in July 1803 and made compromises to maintain his freedom.

Thomas Moore published the first of several highly popular poems on Emmet and Curran in the 1807 volume of *Irish Melodies*. Moore, a childhood friend of Emmet's and fellow Trinity United Irishman, celebrated his comrade's life at a time when explicitly favourable prose items were unlikely to be printed. The emphasis on the romantic aspects of Emmet's story quickly overshadowed his lesser-known experiences as a United Irishmen. The improving political climate exemplified by the granting of Catholic Emancipation in 1829 encouraged ex-United Irishmen Thomas Cloney and Charles Teeling to write accounts of their Rebellion experiences. Neither Cloney nor Teeling was forthcoming regarding his involvement with Emmet, whose subversive 'speech from the dock' engendered an enduring notoriety. Dublin author Joseph Hamilton attempted to correct public misconceptions concerning Emmet and Fitzgerald in 1832. By then Emmet, not yet vindicated by the creation of an Irish republic, was primarily regarded as a tragic/romantic character in popular literature and folk memory.

Democracy advocates within the British Chartist and Young Ireland movements revived the political programme of the United Irishmen in the reform agitation of the 1830s and 1840s. Scorned by the moderate and conservative followers of Daniel O'Connell, as a separatist revolutionary Emmet was accorded equal status with Wolfe Tone by the new Republicans of Young Ireland. Treason felony charges against John Mitchel were defended in May 1848 by Emmet's brother-in-law, Robert Holmes, who made reference in court to the ordeal of his famous relative. The ideals of the United Irishmen, if not also their methods, retained relevance and contributed to the somewhat desperate armed showing of the Young Irelanders in August 1848. The political turmoil and administrative malfunction that typified Anglo-Irish affairs in the mid-1800s had a profound effect on Emmet's status in the historiography of the period. Loyalist historian W.H. Maxwell of Newry was one of the few who dared address the implications of the Rising of 1803 but did so in an inaccurate and cursory fashion in 1845. More importantly, he commissioned George Cruikshank to produce a series of racist caricatures to illustrate his narrative treatment of the Rebellion period. He was motivated, in part, by concern at nationalist mobilisation against Ireland's membership of the United Kingdom. Richard Robert Madden, whose Donnybrook relatives conspired with Emmet, published a series of comprehensive volumes between the 1840s and 1860s charting the history of the United Irishmen. A substantial extract dealing with Robert Emmet appeared in Glasgow in 1847 and represented the first serious attempt at a political biography.

The post-Famine years witnessed a further revival of Emmet's reputation by advanced nationalists who assembled under the banner of the 'Emmet Monument Association' to found the Irish Republican Brotherhood (Fenians). The IRB openly professed adherence to Emmet's militant terms for vindication and garnered massive support for its revolutionary objectives in the early 1860s. The politics of commemoration ensured that the 1878 centenary of Emmet's birth was widely observed by IRB members and sympathisers. Efforts to erect a substantial memorial to the Dubliner, however, stalled owing to financial problems and the difficulty of obtaining permission from Unionist-controlled city administration. Tone's resting-place at Bodenstown, Kildare, became the premier focus of Republican veneration by the turn of the nineteenth century, but great efforts were expended in the advent of the 1903 bicentenary of Emmet's death to identify his unmarked grave. The comparatively subdued 1898 anniversary of the Great Rebellion spurred politically active nationalists to redouble their efforts in 1902–3, when Emmet's life and legacy towered above all others concerned in the Rising of 1803. Fenian icon John O'Leary presided over the major national demonstration in Dublin in September 1903 and addressed a crowd of over 70,000 delegates from all 32 counties and the Irish world.

Pádraig Pearse, Tom Clarke, James Connolly, Sir Roger Casement and other influential Republicans found sufficient common ground in the first decade of the 1900s to cooperate between 1912 and 1916. They located themselves in the same continuum of resistance in which Emmet featured so prominently and fomented the Easter Rising of 1916 in a bid to resurrect Irish sovereignty. The 1916 Proclamation, modelled in part on the 1803 version, referenced the earlier insurrection. Pearse, a fervent admirer of Emmet, also emulated Philip Long's address to the 'Citizens of Dublin' by issuing a document of the same title to the same metropolitan constituency. The executions that followed the suppression of the 1916 Rising and the outbreak of the War of Independence in 1919, however, dramatically altered the context in which Emmet was viewed. Republicans of 1919–21 looked to the 1916 leaders for inspiration, and those of the dispiriting Civil War of 1922–3 revered men who had recently fallen in the struggle against Britain. Similarly, while the IRA and Sinn Féin positively noted the role of the United Irishmen before and during the Border Campaign of 1956–62, it was the immediate, militarily successful precedents of the early twentieth century that dominated their propaganda.

There was little academic interest in Emmet after 1958, when León Ó Broin's short biography addressed several unsustainable theories raised by Helen Landreth in 1949. Access to hitherto closed archives in Dublin and London did not lead to the major reassessment of Emmet's political career that was clearly warranted, indicating satisfaction with the limited insights available. Further examination of a progenitor of armed Republicans was discouraged when conflict took root in the North of Ireland in 1968–70. The ensuing climate of censorship, coupled with the iconoclastic tendencies of 'revisionism' within academia, further degraded the position of Emmet in modern historiography. Events to mark the bicentenary of Emmet's birth in 1978 were largely unofficial, if popular in Dublin's south city. This coolness reflected the perception that the fiftieth anniversary of Easter 1916 had contributed to the resurgence of the IRA. Emmet's name had featured in April 1966, when Jerome Connor's statue of the patriot was unveiled opposite his birthplace. Paradoxically, the ingrained folk memory of Emmet preserved his rare status as a household name into the 1980s, even if something of an enigma. While a new generation of academics began to reassess the United Irishmen, a combination of political and economic circumstances permitted the demolition of Emmet's home in 1984. The more auspicious context of the 2003 bicentenary, however, presented an opportunity for a reassessment of the history and legacy of Robert Emmet.

Robert Emmett [sic] (*Criminal Recorder: or biographical sketches of notorious public characters,* **vol. 1** (London, 1804)).

Robert Emmet **by James Petrie** (NGI, 11,163).

THE

IRISH MAGAZINE,

AND

MONTHLY ASYLUM

FOR

NEGLECTED BIOGRAPHY.

For NOVEMBER, 1808.

We are much concerned, that we are disappointed in our Intention of giving a Likeness of the unfortunate Subject of this Memoir, as some of our Enemies have succeeded in an unfair collusion with the Engraver.

MEMOIRS OF ROBERT EMMETT.

THIS extraordinary and unfortunate youth, was the son of the late Doctor Emmett, a gentleman eminently distinguished for professional skill, and extensive learning, his children inherited the abilities of the father as well as his amiable manners. The eldest son Temple Emmett at 26 years of age, had no rival at the Irish bar for learning, eloquence, and a profound knowledge of his profession. A premature death, in the year 1788, deprived his family and his country of one of the most promising young men that has appeared as a candidate for public favor or judicial distinctions, but his virtues, and the Irish spirit which animated his family, we apprehend would never allow him to earn guilty elevation at the expence of his honor and his country. His brother the celebrated Thomas Addis Emmet, who was educated a physicsan, was called to the bar on the death of Temple, where he rapidly rose by his great talents, and amiable manners to a professional celebrity unknown to be acquired by any man of his time at the bar. His enemies though numerous and vindictive have not presumed to deprive Mr. Emmet of the great reputation he acquired in the opinion of a great and injured people.
3 Q   The

Irish Magazine, **November 1808.**

Although he was spared the indignity of being caricatured by United Irish opponents, articles on Emmet in pro-government publications were generally illustrated by imaginary portraits. Walter Cox, United Irishman and 1803 leader, was initially frustrated in his attempt to procure an engraving of James Petrie's trial portrait. The image subsequently appeared in the February 1809 edition of the journal.

Thomas Moore, **William Brocas** (NLI, 2115 (TX) 82).

137

Sarah Sturgeon (née Curran) to Anne Penrose, January 1808 (NLI, MS 8326).

The poems of Thomas Moore greatly boosted the appeal of Emmet's story in the early to mid-nineteenth century. Moore's focus on the doomed romance between Emmet and Curran was especially emotive, as was her subsequent decline into premature death in Kent, England, on 5 May 1808. Though reputedly painted by Romney, there is no authoritative extant portrait of Curran.

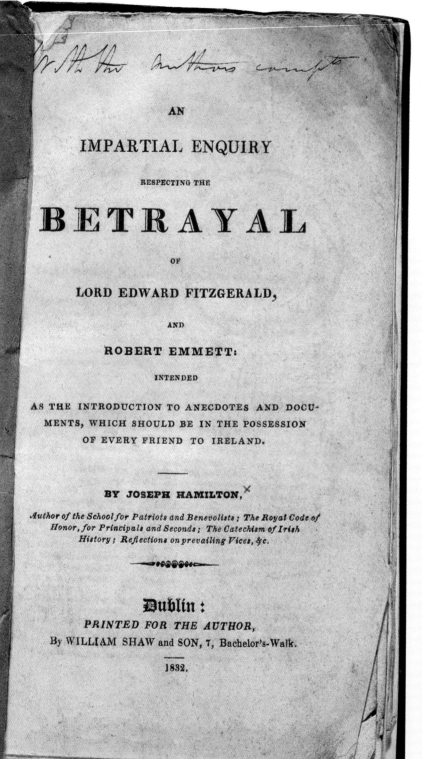

AN

IMPARTIAL ENQUIRY

RESPECTING THE

BETRAYAL

OF

LORD EDWARD FITZGERALD,

AND

ROBERT EMMETT:

INTENDED

AS THE INTRODUCTION TO ANECDOTES AND DOCU-
MENTS, WHICH SHOULD BE IN THE POSSESSION
OF EVERY FRIEND TO IRELAND.

BY JOSEPH HAMILTON,

*Author of the School for Patriots and Benevolists; The Royal Code of
Honor, for Principals and Seconds; The Catechism of Irish
History; Reflections on prevailing Vices, &c.*

Dublin:

PRINTED FOR THE AUTHOR,
By WILLIAM SHAW and SON, 7, Bachelor's-Walk.

1832.

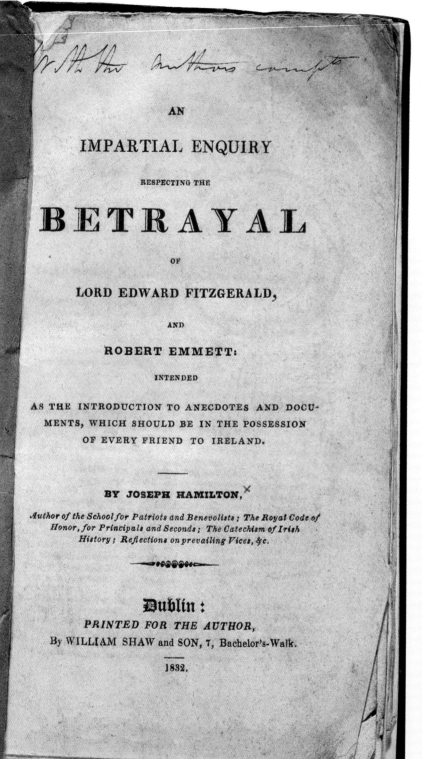

Joseph Hamilton, *An impartial enquiry respecting the betrayal of Lord Edward Fitzgerald, and Robert Emmett [sic]...* (Dublin, 1832).

Hamilton was one of the first historians to interview contemporaries of Robert Emmet with a view to ascertaining the real events underlying received notions of the Rebellion period.

Opposite
'Heroines of Irish history. VI: Sarah Curran at Bully's Acre' (*Irish Fireside*, 12 August 1885)**.**

Emmet's relationship with Curran inspired a story that she had visited Hospital Fields, Kilmainham ('Bully's Acre'), where his remains were interred by the Roscommon Militia on 20 September 1803. This unprestigious burial occurred owing to an oversight whereby Revd Gamble failed to claim the body on behalf of the distraught Mary Anne Emmet.

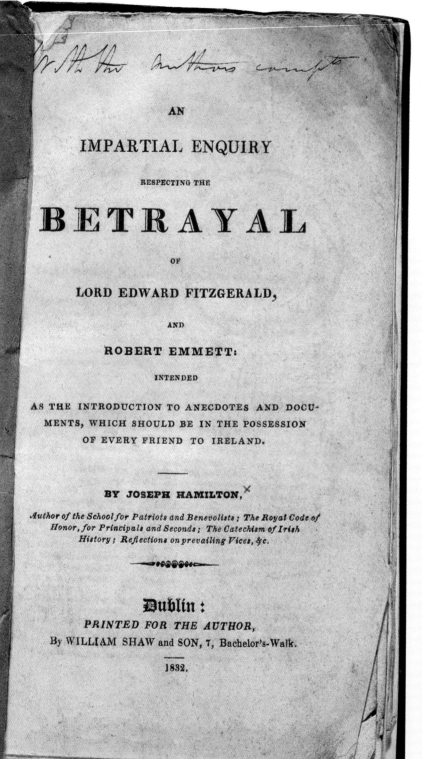

138

EMMET GRAVE AT ST. MICHAN'S.

'Emmet grave at St. Michan's'
(*Evening Telegraph*, 10 October 1891).

'The grave at Old Glasnevin' (*Evening Telegraph*, 10 October 1891).

Revd Gamble and a group of Trinity students evidently reburied Emmet in the grounds of St Michan's, Church Street, on 24 September 1803. They were assisted by the Jacksons of Church Street and Pill Lane, the most prominent United Irish family in the area. Curran was apparently brought to the site by Mrs Archibald Hamilton Rowan, a visit complicated by the maintenance of martial law and her estrangement from her father. Old Glasnevin cemetery and the Hill–Trevor vault in North King Street are two of the most frequently cited alternative sites of Emmet's resting-place.

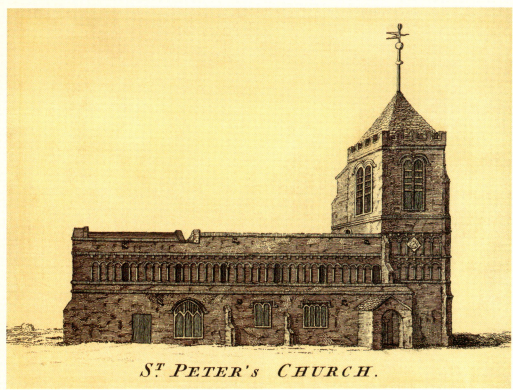

St. Peter's Church
(NLI, 698 TA).

St Peter's, Aungier St. (NGI, 6274).

The death of Mary Anne Emmet on 10 March 1805 provided an opportunity to inter her and her famous brother jointly in the family tomb at St Peter's and St Kevin's, Aungier Street. The unorthodox nature of Mary Anne Emmet's funeral (unlisted, private and nocturnal) supports the provenance of the story averring that Robert Emmet was simultaneously re-interred in accordance with his final wishes. This is further suggested by the central involvement of Revd Gamble, but verification, actively sought by excavations in 1902–3, was frustrated by the obliteration of the tomb during major redevelopment of the church and cemetery in the 1870s.

The illustrious sons of Ireland (NLI, HP (1875) 1).

Emmet was firmly established as one of the most important figures in Irish history by the mid-1800s. Petrie's frontal portrait was typically adapted in preference to the less suitable and less dramatic profiles by Brocas and Comerford.

Robert Emmet, The Irish Patriot by **RSL** (NLI, HP (1798) 43).

143

Robert Emmet, Patriot, in court during his trial by **William Read** (NGI, 10,779).

Rob[er]t Emmet Esqr, from an original portrait drawn and engraved by [James] Petrie (NLI, PD EMME-RO (3) I).

Petrie's 1808 left profile portrait was also much favoured in the late 1800s.

Opposite
Rob[er]t Emmet Esqr **by James Petrie**
(NLI, PD EMME-RO (7) I, (4) I and (5) I).

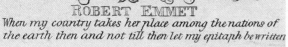

ROBERT EMMET

When my country takes her place among the nations of the earth then and not till then let my epitaph be written

145

Robert Emmet and Norbury (*Weekly Freeman*, 13 December 1902).

The enduring and inspirational appeal of the speech from the dock ensured that it was frequently alluded to during times of nationalist political resurgence.

Opposite

Robert Emmet (NGI, 2363).
This watercolour on paper, an unsigned product of the Irish School, testifies to the huge demand for Emmet illustrations in various media.

**R[ichard] B[rinsley] Sheridan by John Charles Lochée,
stipple by James Heath** (NLI, EP SHER-RI 4).

Nationalist politician and playwright Richard Brinsley Sheridan participated in Westminster debates on the Rising of 1803 and backed unsuccessful calls for a full enquiry. Sheridan privately offered to publicise the case of Anne Devlin, mistreated by Dr Trevor when in Kilmainham Gaol, but was not sufficiently trusted by the

**Right Hon[oura]ble William Conyngham Plunket
by James Heath** (NLI, EP PLUN-WI (3) II).

Wicklowwoman. William Conyngham Plunket had been on friendly terms with Thomas Addis Emmet before 1798. His role in the prosecution of Robert Emmet damaged his reputation and precipitated a series of libel cases arising from printed allegations that the Dubliner had called Plunket a 'viper'.

Richard Robert Madden by G. Mulvany (NLI, EP MADD-RI (2) 1).

R.R. Madden, whose Donnybrook home had been raided on the day of his birth in 1798, developed a lifelong interest in the Rebellion period that complicated his career in the Colonial Office. *The United Irishmen, their lives and times*, a colossal undertaking that occupied Madden for two decades, preserved vital biographical details and political documents that would otherwise have been permanently lost.

The 1803 Depot by George Cruikshank (NLI, HP (1798) 14).

W.H. Maxwell, **engraved by J. Kirkwood** (NLI, EP MAXW-WI (1) 1).

W.H. Maxwell, Unionist, novelist and army officer, disapproved of the United Irishmen and the threat posed by Daniel O'Connell's Repeal Movement to the integrity of the United Kingdom. Cruikshank's misleading illustrations portrayed the rebels as subhuman and murderous. They were reprinted in the 1880s, when the Home Rule issue gained ground in Westminster. The Marshalsea depot did not, in fact, contain a forge, and the weaponry produced was carefully concealed on the premises.

Counsellor [Daniel] O'Connell (NLI, EP OCON-DA (46) 1).

Daniel O'Connell was a member of the Lawyer's Artillery yeomanry in 1803 and raided a house in James's Street in the aftermath of the Rising. A firearm recovered by O'Connell was displayed in his Derrynane home. Although an ex-United Irishman, the Kerryman was appalled by the carnage of 1798 and bitterly resented the death of Lord Kilwarden. He claimed that Emmet would have been forgotten had it not been for public sympathy arising from his association with Sarah Curran.

Design for memorial, Thomas Street (*Young Ireland*, 23 March 1878).

IRB interest in commemorations encouraged a proposal to erect a memorial to Emmet during the 1878 centenary of his birth.

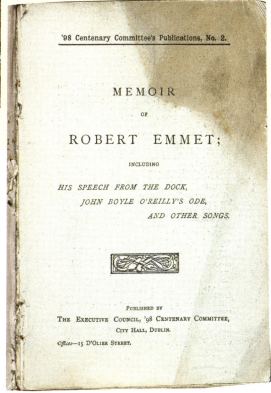

Memoir of Robert Emmet, including his speech from the dock, John Boyle O'Reilly's ode, and other songs (NLI, LO P 76).

Dublin Fenians celebrated Emmet's life in 1869 when news reached the city of the escape of John Boyle O'Reilly from Western Australia to Boston. O'Reilly had been arrested close to St Catherine's Church in Thomas Street, Dublin, and, when safely in America, wrote a poem on Emmet that was republished in Ireland in 1898. He presided over Emmet events in Boston in 1878.

Robert Emmet memorial plate (photographs © Geoffrey Croft/AIHS).

Emmet's diary lock
(photograph © Geoffrey Croft/AIHS).

153

Emmet's champagne glass (photograph © Geoffrey Croft/AIHS).

Emmet's eponymous nephew, former chairman of the Repeal Association in New York, painted and auctioned a commemorative plate in March 1880 to raise money for the Irish Famine Fund. It was acquired by the American Irish Historical Society, which also received Emmet's champagne goblet from Sir Thomas Grattan Esmonde, MP. The society owns a diary lock believed to have been used by Emmet.

Death coming for Lord Norbury (detail) (Dúchas/Emmet family).

Robert Emmet, **artist unknown**
(Dúchas/Emmet family).

A late nineteenth-century American edition of Emmet's speech from the dock was illustrated with a striking image of Lord Norbury being piked by 'death'. The inclusion of Emmet's inscribed tomb implied the inevitable victory of the Republican project and is indicative of the Fenian agenda of its distributors.

ANNE DEVLIN

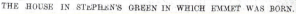

THE HOUSE IN STEPHEN'S GREEN IN WHICH EMMET WAS BORN.

TO
the memory
OF
ANNE DEVLIN
(CAMPBELL)
the faithful servant,
OF
ROBERT EMMET
who possessed some rare
and many noble qualities
who lived in obscurity and poverty
and so died
on the 18th day of Sept: 1851
aged 70 Years

May she rest in peace Amen

Impressions of Emmet's life (NLI, IR 92 E 43). **'House in Stephen's Green', 'Anne Devlin', 'Anne Devlin's monument' and 'Brandon Tynan as Robert Emmet'.**

155

Emmet's position in Irish popular culture was well established by the late 1800s and stimulated interest in several of his associates.

Michael Dwyer (*Irish Emerald*, March 1898).

The association of Wicklow insurgent Michael Dwyer with Robert Emmet was of mutual benefit for their reputations during the centenary celebrations of 1898–1903.

This wall stands over the supposed site of the Emmet Family Vault, which was apparently removed to make room for the foundations of new Transept. Thomas Addis Emmet, M.D. of New York, and other members of the Family have had this brass placed here. ✠ A.D. 1908.

Opposite
The Aungier Street excavations, 1903 (Dúchas/Emmet family).

Emmet family plaque on transept wall of St Peter's and St Kevin's Church (Emmet, *Memoir*).

Dr T.A. Emmet of New York, grandnephew of Robert Emmet, supervised major excavations in search of the family tomb in St Peter's and St Kevin's Church, Aungier Street, in July 1903. It was surmised that the tomb was either overbuilt or destroyed during the laying of the transept foundations in the late 1800s. Dr Emmet arranged the dedication of a plaque inside the church in 1908.

John O'Leary by Ben Bay (NLI, PD 2159 TX (1) 46).

W[illiam] B[utler] Yeats by **John Butler Yeats** (NLI, PD 3099 TX 29).

Ex-Fenian John O'Leary, master of ceremonies during the 1903 centenary in Dublin, interested the Yeats brothers (William and Jack) in Emmet's legacy. John Devoy of Clan na Gael invited W.B. Yeats to address a major gathering of Irish-Americans in the Academy of Music, Brooklyn, on 28 February 1904.

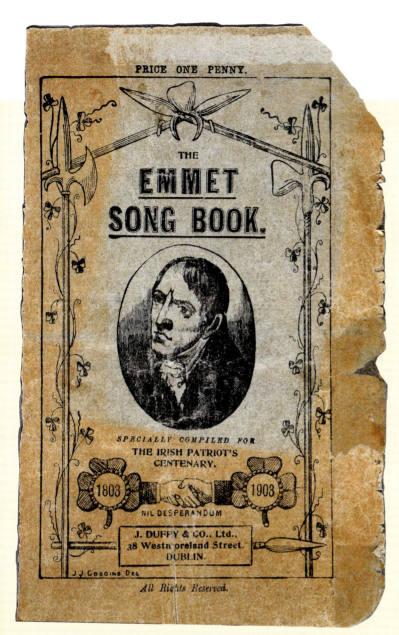

The Emmet songbook, specially compiled for the Irish Patriot's centenary (Dublin, 1903).

Although comparatively few songs were written about Emmet—the best known being 'The last moments of Robert Emmet' (aka 'Bold Robert Emmet') written *c.* 1900 by Tom Maguire—the 1903 centenary encouraged this special compilation.

Report on the centennial celebrations of 20 September 1903 (*Freeman's Journal*, 21 September 1903).

The success of the Dublin demonstrations reinvigorated interest in Emmet's biography and political legacy.

THE EMMET CENTENARY.

Dublin did well yesterday. Robert Emmet was a Dublin man, and it was fitting that the celebration of his Centenary should have been participated in in an especial way by the men of Dublin. It was Dublin men who, first and last, gave their support to his daring scheme of seizing Dublin Castle; and, with the Wicklow contingent, it was Dublin men who made the supreme effort to put the scheme into practice. But that, after all, was only a detail of the influence which brought together yesterday in the streets of Dublin the tens of thousands of people who gathered to pay their tribute to the young martyr who, just a hundred years previously, expiated on the scaffold the crime of loving his country—not wisely, some would say, but too well; but we say both wisely and well. And why? The blood of the martyrs, it is said, is the seed of the Church; and the blood of Emmet, as it flowed in Thomas street a hundred years ago, has fructified in many a young Irish mind since, at home and abroad, to the glory and the credit and the practical benefit of Ireland. There are people who sneer at Robert Emmet's attempt to subvert the British power in Ireland as the foolish dash of a brainless and enthusiastic boy; but those who have studied the details of his plan know that it was thought out with wonderful precision, and, so far as it was tactically and strategically sound, we have the opinion of a leading British General, still alive, that it could not have been improved upon. Why is it that Robert Emmet is such a unique figure in this heroic period of Irish history? Wolfe Tone was a leader and patriot of consummate courage and ability. Wellington, indeed, years after 'Ninety-Eight described him as the most formidable enemy England had had to deal with in his time, except Napoleon. Lord Edward, again, was a trained soldier, and the scion of a great and historic house. Yet there can scarcely be a doubt that, amongst the three men, notwithstanding Davis's "Sainted Edward," and his "Wolfe Tone's Grave," the one whose memory is sweetest and dearest to-day to the Irish people is Robert Emmet. Is it his youth? That, we think, has something to do with it. But M'Cracken was young also, and Munro was young, and Father Murphy was young. And if Emmet loved Sarah Curran did not Lord Edward love Pamela; and did not many a true husband leave the wife or the sweetheart he adored in that dread year for the sake of the deathless cause he believed in? There is something in Emmet's youth, there is something in his affection for the daughter of Philpot Curran, to explain the peculiar poignancy with which Irishmen a hundred years afterwards regard his fate. But there is a bigger and a greater motive at work. In his Ode, written in 1878, on the Centenary of Emmet's birth, John Boyle O'Reilly cried, in his opening line, "Tear down the crape from the column"! There was no crape yesterday. There were no flags flying half-mast. It was not a dead cause that was being celebrated, but a cause resurgent. Why, we ask again, is Emmet to-day so great a figure in the Irish imagination? Is it not because, when all had been lost—when his brother and his friends had been scattered, some to dungeons, some into exile, some to the grave—when the doors of the Irish Parliament had been closed with the rusty key of corruption—when the memory of 'Ninety-Eight and the memory of the Dead were spoken about in whispers along Thomas street and the back alleys of the Liberties—is it not because, in this deepest and dismallest hour of gloom, this young Trinity student stepped out with his immortal torch and lit the darkness? Yes; that is the greatness of Robert Emmet. His scheme may have been a good one or a bad one. On that question even Irish Nationalists may agree to differ. But they cannot differ as to the greatness of the man's soul, or as to the superb example he has given to his countrymen. It is a trite thing to say that nothing effectual can be done, for nations or for men, except at some sacrifice. That is a truism universally accepted. But what Emmet taught us—and perhaps the lesson was needed, even in his day, and it is needed now—was that we must persevere, even under the most discouraging circumstances, if we hope ever to win. Nor is it any exaggeration, we think, to say that the present generation has profited by the lesson. In the poem to which we have already referred John Boyle O'Reilly dates the beginning of Irish reform from the Tone and Emmet epoch. It is a true reading of Irish history. They sowed the seed. And it was fit thus Dublin and

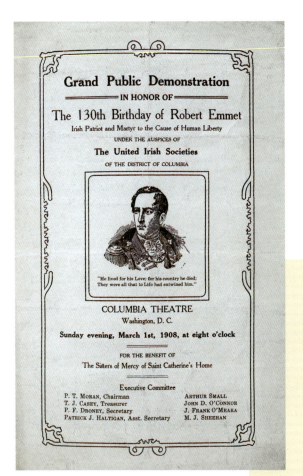

'Grand public demonstration in honor of the 130th birthday of Robert Emmet, Irish patriot and martyr to the cause of human liberty, under the auspices of the United Irish Societies of the District of Columbia…March 1st, 1908'.

Emmet anniversary celebration, Round Room, Rotunda, 5 March 1906.

Emmet's date of birth and execution were observed in many Irish centres and in preference to the anniversary of the Rising of 1803, which, much misunderstood, was deemed neither glorious nor impressive.

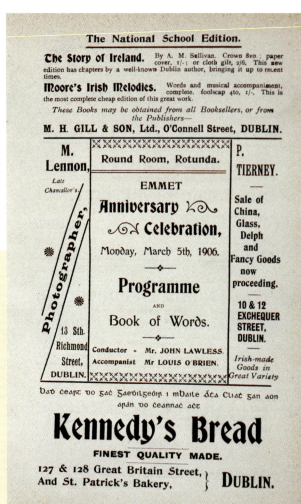

Opposite
Wolfe Tone Memorial Committee, Emmet Anniversary Celebration…Round Room, Rotunda, 4th March 1915, programme pages.

Arthur Griffith, a vocal protagonist during the 1903 centenary, maintained his interest in Emmet after founding Sinn Féin. IRB leader Tom Clarke also supported the Rotunda celebration. The foundation of the nationalist Irish Volunteer movement in Ireland and gun-running incidents at Howth, Co. Dublin, and Kilcoole, Co. Wicklow, in July and August 1914 strengthened the hand of those demanding the enactment of the Home Rule Bill.

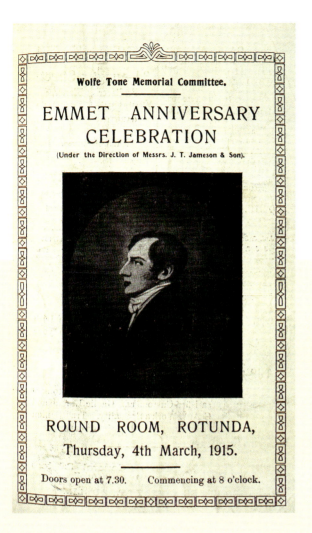

Wolfe Tone Memorial Committee.

EMMET ANNIVERSARY CELEBRATION

(Under the Direction of Messrs. J. T. Jameson & Son).

ROUND ROOM, ROTUNDA,
Thursday, 4th March, 1915.

Doors open at 7.30.   Commencing at 8 o'clock.

NOTICE.

THE Wolfe Tone Memorial Association acknowledge its indebtedness to Mr. Patrick Mahon, who, in spite of great difficulties occasioned by the seizure of his machinery by the military and police on Tuesday, 2nd inst, has succeeded in turning out this programme and regret that the words of a song—"The Day"—by Brian na Banban, specially written for the occasion, together with other appropriate poems & articles, had of necessity to be omitted.

161

'I CONFIDENTLY AND ASSUREDLY HOPE THAT THERE IS STILL UNION AND STRENGTH IN IRELAND' — Rob* Emmet

THE ADMONITION OF A PATRIOT.

'The admonition of a patriot' (*Irish World*, 13 March 1915).

'Rush for the special number' (*Gaelic American*, 13 March 1915).

The *Gaelic American* of 6 March 1915, organ of Devoy's IRB-affiliated Clan na Gael organisation, comprised a 'special Emmet anniversary number'. Emmet's legacy was also cited by the rival *Irish World*, which depicted the Dubliner criticising the splitting of the Volunteers into a faction that supported John Redmond's call to enlist in the army and the IRB-controlled minority that opposed the initiative. Tom Clarke and Pádraig Pearse were among those executed in the aftermath of the ensuing 1916 Rising.

RUSH FOR THE SPECIAL NUMBER

The demand for the special Emmet anniversary number of the Gaelic American has been so great that we had to go to press twice during the past week.

A limited number of copies can be obtained up to March 17 at 5 cents each. After that date the price of any copies of the special number which may remain unsold will be 10 cents each.

Robert Emmet, a commemorative booklet, 1921 (Dublin, 1921).

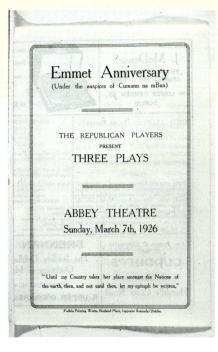

'Emmet Anniversary, under the auspices of Cumann na mBan', 1926 (NLI, Abbey programmes, Ir 3919 A1).

The rise of physical force Republicanism between 1916 and 1923 stimulated frequent references to Emmet and fundraising events held in his honour.

1803 and 1916 (Kilmainham).

Albert Power memorial, Harold's Cross (photograph by David Monaghan).

Officers of the IRA's Old Fourth Battalion, Dublin Brigade, commissioned Albert Power, RHA, to execute a bas-relief of Emmet on Robert Emmet Bridge, Harold's Cross. The location was close to the subsequently demolished Palmer house, in which Emmet had been arrested. An appeal for funds was issued in October 1938 by Oscar Traynor, Frank Thornton and John Dowling, former enemies during the Civil War.

Ref.: S.139

bᴜʀᴏ ꜱᴛᴀɪʀᴇ ᴍɪʟᴇᴀᴛᴀ 1913-21
(Bureau of Military History 1913-21)

QUESTIONNAIRE

on

**The Rising of Easter Week 1916
and Associated Events**

To Mr John Hanratty

This questionnaire is the property of the Bureau. Any statement or information given on any matter with which it deals will be treated as confidential.

26 Westland Row,
Dublin

'Phone: 61018

7. To what extent, if any, was it inspired by that of Robert Emmet?

8. Did the plan contemplate immobilisation in buildings?

   If not, was such immobilisation the result of the Countermanding Order or what was the purpose?

The Bureau of Military History, founded in 1947 by Oscar Traynor when Minister for Defence, interviewed IRA veterans in relation to the perceived links between the risings of 1803 and 1916.

Cork Irish Republican Army leader Michael Collins signed bonds of the unrecognised Irish government in 1919 on the block used in Emmet's decapitation. This was a significant act of identification which that complemented the choice of venue, St. Enda's, Rathfarnham, where Pearse had founded his progressive Irish school.

DÁIL ÉIREANN

DÍOSPÓIREACHTA PARLAIMINTE
PARLIAMENTARY DEBATES

TUAIRISC OIFIGIÚIL
OFFICIAL REPORT

IMLEABHAR 137.   VOLUME 137.

Dé Céadaoin 11ú Márta, 1953.
Wednesday, 11th March, 1953.

Do chuaigh an Ceann Comhairle igceannas ar 2 p.m.

Ceisteanna—Questions.
Oral Answers.

Newspaper Leading Article.

Mr. Briscoe asked the Taoiseach whether his attention has been drawn to a leading article in a Dublin evening newspaper of 27th February, 1953, which said that Robert Emmet's insurrection was a miserable affair, a tragic farce that was squashed in a few hours, and that he exerted no influence on the story of Ireland; and, if so, whether he will take steps, if necessary by the introduction of proposals for legislation, to prevent anti-national attacks such as this on Irish patriots.

Parliamentary Secretary to the Taoiseach (Donnchadh ó Briain) (for the Taoiseach): I have seen the article to which the Deputy refers. I do not think it necessary to take any such steps as he suggests.

The reputation of Robert Emmet, like that of the other patriots who gave their lives in efforts to secure the freedom of our country, is safe in the affections of the people.

Mr. Briscoe: Is the Taoiseach aware that the paper is the *Evening Mail,* which has a wide circulation mainly amongst our young people and can influence wrongly the minds of people

in matters of this kind? If steps cannot be taken, surely that paper should not receive Government support in the shape of advertisements?

General Mulcahy: Is the Taoiseach aware of the way in which newspapers in this country are insistently and persistently attacking the memory of men like Griffith and Collins?

An Ceann Comhairle: That is a separate question.

Dáil debate, 11 March 1953
(*Parliamentary Debates*, Official Report, vol. 137).

The iconic status of Emmet in Irish society ensured that his legacy was occasionally the subject of Civil War-related rivalry during the 150th anniversary of his death. Stamps in 1/3d (red) and 3d (green) denominations were released in 1953. The first day of issue, 21 September, was inappropriate given that Emmet was executed on 20 September. This anomaly arose as the anniversary fell on a Sunday, when post offices were closed.

165

Emmet commemorative stamp, 1953 (An Post, *Postage stamps of Ireland* (Dublin, 1992)).

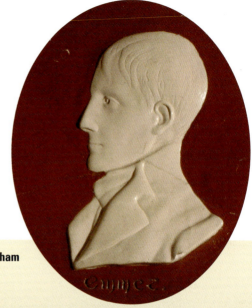

Left
Bust of Emmet in Trinity College, Dublin (photograph by David Monaghan).

Right
Emmet relief in Kilmainham (Kilmainham).

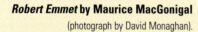
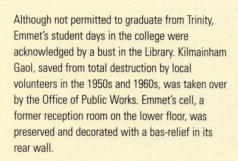

Robert Emmet by Maurice MacGonigal
(photograph by David Monaghan).

Although not permitted to graduate from Trinity, Emmet's student days in the college were acknowledged by a bust in the Library. Kilmainham Gaol, saved from total destruction by local volunteers in the 1950s and 1960s, was taken over by the Office of Public Works. Emmet's cell, a former reception room on the lower floor, was preserved and decorated with a bas-relief in its rear wall.

167

**Painted plaster statuette of Emmet.
Attributed to 'Bachman'** (photograph ©
Geoffrey Croft/AIHS).

The search for Emmet's body (Dúchas/Emmet family).

The final major investigation into the location of Emmet's remains concentrated on the Hill–Trevor vault in North King Street, Dublin, in 1966. It was established that a skeleton preserved in an apple box was not that of the patriot leader.

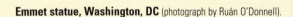

Emmet statue, St Stephen's Green (NLI).

Emmet statue, Washington, DC (photograph by Ruán O'Donnell).

An American delegation that included Timothy 'Tip' O'Neill presented a copy of Jerome Connor's bronze of Emmet to the Irish nation on 13 April 1966. It was sited across the road from Emmet's birthplace until 2002, when the building of the Luas light railway led to its relocation within St Stephen's Green. Connor produced the first of three casts of the figure in Washington, DC, in 1917. Eamon De Valera unveiled one in Golden Gate Park, San Francisco, when on a fundraising tour of America in July 1919. A second had been dedicated in the Smithsonian Institution, Washington, DC, and removed to a more public location on Massachusetts Avenue on 22 April 1966. The fourth was commissioned by the Ancient Order of Hibernians and erected in Emmetsburg, Iowa, in 1958.

Lithographic portrait of Robert Emmet by Thomas Kelly, New York, 1874 (photograph © Geoffrey Croft/AIHS).

Emmet memorial coin (Kilmainham).

The town of Emmetsburg, Iowa, was founded by Irish emigrants after the Great Famine.

Further reading

Agnew, Jean (ed.), *The Drennan–McTier letters*, 3 vols (Dublin, 1998–9).

Byrne, Miles, *Memoirs of Miles Byrne*, 2 vols (Dublin, 1906).

Carroll, Denis, *The man from God knows where: Thomas Russell, 1767–1803* (Dublin, 1995).

Chambers, Liam, *Rebellion in Kildare, 1790–1803* (Dublin, 1998).

Dickson, Charles, *The life of Michael Dwyer* (Dublin, 1944).

Elliott, Marianne, *Partners in revolution: the United Irishmen and France* (London, 1982).

Emmet, T.A., *Memoir of Thomas Addis Emmet and Robert Emmet*, 2 vols (New York, 1915).

Finegan, John (ed.), *Anne Devlin, patriot and heroine* (Dublin, 1968; reprinted Dublin 1992).

Geoghegan, Patrick M., *Robert Emmet, a life* (Dublin, 2002).

MacDonagh, Michael (ed.), *The viceroy's post bag* (London, 1904).

Madden, R.R., *Robert Emmet* (Glasgow, 1847).

Madden, R.R., *The United Irishmen, their lives and times*, 2nd edn, 4 vols (Dublin, 1857–60).

Newsinger, John (ed.), *United Irishman: the autobiography of James Hope* (London, 2001).

Ó Brádaigh, Seán, *Bold Robert Emmet, 1778–1803* (Dublin, 2003).

Ó Broin, León, *The unfortunate Mr Robert Emmet* (Dublin, 1958).

O'Donnell, Ruán, *Aftermath: post-Rebellion insurgency in Wicklow, 1799–1803* (Dublin, 2000).

O'Donnell, Ruán, *Robert Emmet and the Rebellion of 1798* (Dublin, 2003).

O'Donnell, Ruán, *Robert Emmet and the Rising of 1803* (Dublin, 2003).

Quinn, James, *Soul on fire, a life of Thomas Russell* (Dublin, 2002).

Reynolds, J.J., *Footprints of Emmet* (Dublin, 1903).

Whelan, Kevin, *Fellowship of freedom: the United Irishmen and 1798* (Cork, 1998).

Index

People and places mentioned in the text and captions